P9-BYL-617

Witches and Witch-hunts

MILTON MELTZER

Witches and Witch-hunts

A HISTORY OF PERSECUTION

THE BLUE SKY PRESS
An Imprint of Scholastic Inc.

THE BLUE SKY PRESS

Library of Congress catalog card number: 97-36999
10 9 8 7 6 5 4 3 2 1 9/9 0/0 01 02 03 04
ISBN 0-590-48517-2
Designed by Kathleen Westray
Printed in the United States of America 23
First printing, September 1999

ALSO BY MILTON MELTZER

Carl Sandburg: A Biography

Langston Hughes: A Biography

Lincoln in His Own Words

Frederick Douglass in His Own Words

Slavery: A World History

Ten Queens: Portraits of Women of Power

Weapons and Warfare:
From the Stone Age to the Space Age

A Thoreau Profile
(WITH WALTER HARDING)

The Many Lives of Andrew Carnegie

Dorothea Lange: A Photographer's Life

Contents

Introduction

WITCHES, witches, witches! Were they once everywhere? Are they still harming innocent people with their evil deeds? Public records from the past are full of horrifying tales. Even now, from time to time, the media report on strange practices of present-day witches. Why do stories about witches have such power?

Belief in witchcraft has existed in all lands, from the earliest times to today. In the folklore of peoples almost everywhere, it is believed that certain members of the community harm others by supernatural means. Witches are said to predict the future, to be invulnerable, to have super strength, to transform themselves or others, to fly, to become invisible or cause others to become so. They can make objects move without touching them or produce at will anything desired. Their spells and magic potions can make people fall in love — or even make them die.

A community that believes in witchcraft may persecute individuals. Such persecution may even lead to a mass hysteria that can devastate great numbers. In England, the seventeenth century was a time when the arts and sciences flourished. Nevertheless, even educated people believed in Satan and his handmaidens, the witches. In that atmosphere, almost anyone was fair game for persecution as a witch.

As we will see, a witchcraft craze lasting more than four hundred years — from the fourteenth through the seventeenth centuries — caused the deaths of millions in Europe, the great majority of them women. The craze arose in the Middle Ages and lasted well into the Age of Reason. Long after, in the twentieth century, the Nazi dictator, Adolf Hitler, led an organized campaign of persecution — often called a witch-hunt — of the Jews in Germany and Europe that led to the deaths of six million men, women, and children.

Scientists who have studied the phenomenon of witchcraft say it often has to do with people's ideas about how everyday events can be explained. Among preliterate, so-called primitive societies, the course of events is explained in terms of a basic belief in witchcraft. Believers in witchcraft tend not to be satisfied by an explanation of *how* a certain event occurred if it does not tell them *why* it occurred. For example, if a woman's husband suffers a misfortune that is the result of an observable event, such as being crippled by a trampling elephant, the woman knows *how* that disaster happened. But she looks to witchcraft to tell her *why* the elephant injured *her* husband, and not some other man.

She wants to stop that evil from doing more harm. She may use medicine against it, which may stop the witchcraft and possibly kill the witch. Or she may call in a diviner to find out who the witch is, so that the witch can be put out of business or obliged to remove her witchcraft. She looks for the witch among the people she thinks wish her family harm. She goes to a witch doctor, who knows the local gossip about who hates whom and provides the names of the enemies of his client. And the woman fixes on some definite person whom she thinks has reason to wish her husband harm.

Anthropologists studying communities that believe in witchcraft find that a person often accuses not someone who hates him or envies him, but someone *he* hates or envies. Charges of witchcraft are influenced by personal relations and quarrels. A farmer produces good crops while his neighbors' harvests are poor. A father has a large, healthy family while all around is sickness. A fisherman or a hunter prospers much more than his fellows. Such fortunate people are sometimes believed to achieve their success by witchcraft, at the expense of their neighbors. As one observer of a tribal group in Africa put it,

> the Zande knows that if he becomes rich, the poor will hate him; that if he rises in social position, his inferiors will be jealous of his authority; that if he is handsome, the less favored will envy his looks; that if he is talented as a hunter, singer, a fighter, or a rhetorician, he will earn the malice of those less gifted; and that if he enjoys the regard of his prince and of his neighbors, he will be detested for his prestige and popularity.

In our modern Western society, if an auto accident occurs, there are recognized ways to find out *how* it happened. But we know there is no concrete explanation for *why* it happened to this person and not someone else. We understand the role chance plays in the intersection of chains of events. The Zande and other believers, however, want answers to both questions: HOW and WHY. They believe there are no accidents.

Let's see how commonly held beliefs mesh with personal relationships in a society of an altogether different time and place. . . .

Chapter One

THEY FLY THROUGH THE AIR

IN THE YEAR 1566, in the town of Chelmsford, England, the widow Agnes Waterhouse was held in prison on the charge of witchcraft. A wrinkled old woman with a bowed back and pockmarked face, she had suffered long days of hunger and fear, confined alone in a bleak cell. At last, her spirit broken, she confessed to the many evils she was charged with.

She said she had caused her cat — a creature with baleful eyes and spotted fur, which she called Satan — to do harm to her neighbors. When one of them accused her of witchcraft, she said, she took her cat to the neighbor's house on a moonless night and set Satan free in the hogpen. At sunrise three hogs were dead. And the cat? He was home sleeping peacefully in his basket. For doing her bidding, Agnes rewarded Satan by making a deep scratch in her cheek and giving him the trickle of blood to drink.

Everyone knew Agnes had quarreled with her neighbor, the widow Goodday. So, she confessed, she had told Satan she wished the widow's cow would drown and her flock of geese be ruined. The next day, the cow was found dead, floating in the river. And the geese, with bloody beaks and torn feathers, were squawking wildly in their coop. Again, when Satan returned home, Agnes pricked her cheek and fed the blood to the cat. Look, she said to the court, as she touched her cheek, see where the sore is still festering?

Then a young girl appeared in court. She testified that Agnes had ordered Satan to spoil the brewing of hops, to turn the butter sour in the churn, and to wither the crops in the fields. Ah, said the magistrates, now we know the cause of all these disasters.

It was common knowledge that Agnes and her husband were always fighting. Now Agnes told the court that Satan had helped her to make her husband sick and hasten him to his grave. Since that time — nine years ago — she had lived alone, in poverty.

Poor and hungry, Agnes had gone to a neighboring couple to beg for food. When they slammed their door on her, she had vowed that harm would befall them.

Not many days later, both the husband and wife died of the bloody flux.

Hearing such testimony, the court knew what to do. Agnes was convicted of witchcraft and was hanged on the gallows. She may have been the first woman in England to be executed for witchcraft.

Some of the elements in this English account of a witchcraft case are similar to reports about tribal groups in Africa. There are misfortunes in the community: a cow lost, geese harmed, crops spoiled, butter ruined, a husband and wife dying. And the woman accused of causing all this through witchcraft is old and ugly. She quarrels with her neighbors and fights with her husband. The town's disasters are blamed on a disagreeable, cantankerous old woman. Thrown into jail, she is placed in solitary confinement and starved until her spirit is broken. By now, she is ready to confess to anything to end her agony. The court, believing in witchcraft, convicts her and hangs her.

From many tales, it appears that witchcraft is thought to involve a bargain with the Devil that a person makes in order to gain the power to do harm. A witch is a person who can do or seems to do strange things, beyond the natural, by striking a bargain with evil spirits.

In the Christian world, witchcraft has been considered both a sin and a crime: a sin because it denies that God is supreme, and a crime because once a person makes a deal with the Devil, that person has the power to call on the Evil One. The Evil One would appear in the witch's own shape to perform crimes ranging from theft and the destruction of property to assault and even murder.

Examining the records of witchcraft trials we can gather what people believed — and many still believe — to be the habits and methods of witches:

- Witches operate at night.
- Witches in Europe fly through the air on broomsticks; witches in Central Africa fly on saucer-shaped winnowing baskets.
- Witches employ animal assistants called familiars, such as cats, dogs, and weasels in Europe; dogs and foxes in Japan; hyenas, owls, and baboons in Africa.
- Witches steal or destroy property.
- Witches injure people in many ways: eating their victims while they are still alive, or killing them first and digging up the bodies for ghoulish feasts.

How does one recognize a witch? By any one of such proofs as these:

- Witches possess magic wands, staffs, or rods.
- Witches can't cry; at most they shed three tears.

- Witches have a birthmark under the armpit or hidden elsewhere under hair.
- Witches have to stop when they see a broom to count the straws, or are compelled to count seeds, grain, the holes in a sieve, or letters in a piece of writing.

What do witches look like? It all depends upon where they've been seen — or imagined. There is no one image that fits all communities. Most often, the witch is pictured as female, but in many places, witch tales involve both males and females. Beyond gender, witches are portrayed in many varied ways, from the thin and gaunt in Europe to the very fat — from eating human flesh — in Central Africa.

The question of how beliefs in witches and witchcraft developed has given psychologists and social scientists much to think about. Most people would agree that human beings need to feel secure. We like order in our lives, and we hate chaos. Good government is supposed to keep order and prevent chaos. Yet every society is threatened by human enemies from within and without and by catastrophes — earthquakes, landslides, fire and flood, plague, drought, storms — that some people feel are not part of the natural order.

That fear of disorder has shaped ideas of evil. Whatever threatens order tends to be considered evil. As far back in time as we can trace, people have believed that supernatural powers menace or prey upon us. Satan and his legions of lesser demons are examples. In the ancient world there were many dangerous figures — evil gods, evil spirits, evil ghosts, vampires, dragons, weird monsters. . . . Their existence was taken for granted. While no one had met them in the flesh, few doubted their presence in the underworld or in hell, or that they hid in the dark, lurking in shadows and caves.

People in many places have believed that such sinister forces and beings lie behind suffering, pain, loss, and death. These forces are part of how the world works. A reality of everyday life, they are woven into religion and folk beliefs.

Witchcraft, then, is but one aspect of popular and widespread ideas about the powers of evil. Belief in witches, then or now, owes much to people's fears of what they don't understand. Many people do not believe that chance plays an unavoidable part in human affairs. If something bad happens to them, they tend to blame it on the supernatural powers of witches.

Chapter Two

A WORLD FULL OF DANGERS

THERE ARE innumerable examples of the hold witches have on the imagination. In the Old Testament of the Bible, the celebrated Witch of Endor was consulted by King Saul. The Book of Ezekiel tells of certain women who used magic to control other people. These women were often attacked for going against God and his power and were threatened with the punishment of death. The books of Leviticus and Deuteronomy warn against witches and demand that good people have nothing to do with them.

In the New Testament, Jesus often demonstrated his divine powers of casting out demons. In Christian literature from the New Testament on, Christian missionaries advanced mainly by exposing humankind's invisible enemies, the demons, and driving them out.

The ancient Greeks and Romans believed that magical practices could be good or bad. Practices intended to do harm were condemned and punished, but helpful sorcery was approved. These cultures believed witches could hurt people in various ways — in their business affairs, in politics, in athletics, in love and marriage. They could even cause death.

Some of the Greek and Roman goddesses, such as Diana and Hecate, were thought to perform evil magic at night through various rituals and spells. Hecate was frequently invoked in magic spells. She was the goddess of blood, terror, and witchcraft. She wandered among tombs and drank the blood of corpses. She could harm the living with nightmares and madness. She even made dogs shiver with fright.

Lucius Apuleius, a Roman of the second century A.D., wrote a novel called *The Golden Ass*. It tells of the witches of Thessaly — a place notorious for its witch population — who had the habit of gnawing off bits of a dead man's face to use in their magic and who could transform themselves into animal shapes to carry out their ghoulish purposes.

Witches even exercised magic power over the forces of nature, according to Greek and Roman writers. They could make the sea boil on a windless day, halt a waterfall, or even throw the earth off center. Through such fantastic deeds they reversed the natural order, turning the whole world upside down.

In Homer's epic poem the *Odyssey*, we read of Circe, the witch or sorceress. Her siren song lured Odysseus's crew to her island. There she played upon their weaknesses by offering magical food and drink, such lavish hospitality that her victims could not refuse it.

She made the men feel special by seating them on thrones. She fed them a rich meal and had them drink wine laced with a magical potion that made them lose all thought of their homeland or the desire to return there. They ate and drank so immoderately that they began to look like pigs, and Circe shut them up in a pigsty. It was only with the help of Hermes, the god of travelers, that Odysseus was able to break the spell of Circe and free his men.

Witchcraft figures in Roman literature, too. Virgil, a Roman poet, created the national epic called the *Aeneid*, in which a witch stops the flow of rivers, reverses the stars' courses, and brings trees marching down hillsides.

As the Roman Empire began to crumble and fall, the Germanic invaders spread through Europe. They believed in witches and feared them. Their gods were at times sponsors of witchcraft and at other times victims of it. Women especially were believed to have supernatural powers.

The Nordic religion, like the Greek and Roman, had many gods. Odin was the Supreme One, a demonic, pitiless figure, the god of war. He knew witchcraft and sorcery and stopped at nothing to master knowledge of all mysteries. One ancient Norse people, called the Vikings, who held power from around 800 to 1100 A.D., used a form of writing called runes. Carved in stone or wood, runes held secret meanings bound up with witchcraft. Runes were used not only to attract the opposite sex but also for more deadly ends.

In the medieval era, the Christian church and the state adopted laws against witchcraft practices and beliefs. Charlemagne, the emperor of the West from 800 to 814, condemned witchcraft as so evil a pursuit that its practitioners deserved death. Christian burial was denied to witches. If any had been buried by mistake, they had to be dug up again and burned.

But the church was conflicted. Sometimes its leaders said witchcraft was mere superstition, an illusion, a disgusting hangover from paganism. But at other times they said it was real and had to be crushed.

In the story of Job in the Bible, Satan — or the Devil — destroyed Job's servants and cattle with fire from the skies and killed Job's children with the violent wind that blew their house down on them. Were these disasters real, or an illusion? St. Augustine, the important church leader of the sixth century A.D., said they were concrete disasters caused by demons. While these evil spirits could make people believe in illusions, they could also bring about actual misfortune.

In the history of witchcraft, this was an important argument. It meant that anything popularly blamed on witches, no matter how improbable, could be taken as real. Witches could do almost anything because they were in league with the Devil.

As one scholar writing of the beliefs of the Middle Ages put it, "Witches could kill people by magic. They could make men impotent and women barren. They could ruin harvests, blight men and crops and cattle with disease, steal the milk from cows. They could drive people mad by sending evil spirits into their bodies. They could turn themselves into hares or hedgehogs or balls of string or anything they liked. They could fly through the air, shrieking and cackling, mounted on demonic animals or broomsticks, wisps of straw, sieves, or eggshells."

Again, we can see how, in a world full of dangers beyond their control, people's fears and insecurities made it possible for them to believe in all sorts of supernatural causes and consequences. And to turn against others with devastating effects.

Chapter Three

LADY ALICE OF KILKENNY TOWN

YOU COULD SAY that Lady Alice Kyteler had everything: She was an aristocrat, she was rich, and she was beautiful. Her family were bankers in the town of Kilkenny, Ireland, part of England's domain in the fourteenth century. As a young girl, Lady Alice proved so bright that her father took her into his banking business, an extremely unusual move in an age when women rarely participated in business. At the bank, Lady Alice learned that money had the power to do good or evil.

Early on, she found that her beauty attracted men. By age sixteen she was married, but to a man more interested in her wealth than in Alice herself. He died within six months. Three more husbands followed, one soon after another, and each died an untimely death. One child resulted from those marriages, a son named William, an arrogant, wild fellow who frequently avoided legal charges only by using his mother's influence and money.

Ugly rumors began to spread. Was Alice playing with witchcraft? How could so many husbands die so soon? Wasn't a tall, dark man seen visiting her house at night? Could it be that William was not the son of an earthly father? Yes, many concluded, the Devil himself was Alice's lover.

Lady Alice employed only one servant, a woman named Petronilla. Many thought it strange that such a wealthy woman could manage with only one servant when those with a fraction of her money had many servants. Poor Petronilla suffered many dark looks and sly whispers whenever she went to market.

Still, no one challenged Lady Alice openly. Until one day, in May of 1324, a neighbor across the street from the Kyteler house woke just before dawn. Hearing a strange noise in the street, he opened his shutters to a strange sight. There was Lady Alice, fully dressed, sweeping the cobblestones with a large kitchen broom. But instead of pushing the dirt and debris away from her, she pushed it toward her own house and right into her hallway. She seemed to be muttering something. Listening hard, the neighbor heard her saying, "To the house of William, my son, come all the wealth of Kilkenny town."

And then, "To the house of William, my son, come all the health of Kilkenny town."

Shivering at this weird prayer, the neighbor crept back into bed, believing he had witnessed something no human was meant to see or hear.

Soon after, curious events began to happen in the town. Prosperous businesspeople went bankrupt. Gold, jewels, and other valuables thought to be hidden in safe places suddenly disappeared. Even the beggars and rats of Kilkenny fled the town.

A thick blanket of gloom settled over Kilkenny's people. Something terrible, yet invisible, was threatening them all. So the mayor took it up with the bishop. "As long as I am bishop," said his lordship, "witches will not survive in this place! Didn't it say in Deuteronomy that those who practiced the evil arts were not to be tolerated among the faithful?"

The bishop excommunicated Lady Alice, her son, and her servant, cutting them off from all connection with the Church. And he did it publicly, in front of the great crowd of townspeople who cheered him on. Now they knew their suspicions were right.

Next, Lady Alice, William, and Petronilla were arrested and put in jail to await trial by a judge from Dublin. On the day of the trial, the court was packed, especially with those who thought they had suffered loss or injury from the dark deeds of the accused.

The clerk of the court read out a long list of the crimes Lady Alice was accused of. Then the judge asked her, "What defense do you make against these charges?" But not a word did the proud Lady Alice utter in answer to this or to any of the questions that followed.

"You had better speak up," warned the judge, "for you stand in mortal danger." And he held up a square of black cloth, signifying the presence of witchcraft. "You must know what this means," he said. If she did, she gave no answer, only stared coldly back.

"Don't force my hand," the judge said, "for if I pronounce you a witch, your doom is sealed. Admit to your evil doings while there is time — then perhaps you may earn mercy and forgiveness."

But she only smiled.

At this, the judge pronounced the sentence: one week from this day, Lady Alice would be taken from jail to the place of public execution. The guards moved in to take Alice back to her dungeon. But before they could touch her, she spoke boldly to the crowd: "Do not think that you will see my death a week hence, you who have come here to see this sport!"

The same sentence was passed on Petronilla, despite her claim of innocence. But William was not condemned to death. He denied any knowledge of his mother's wicked deeds, condemned her for them, and promised compensation to all who claimed she had harmed them. The judge ordered the charge of witchcraft against William to be dropped and fined him a huge sum, enough to buy the lead needed to repair the decaying roof of the cathedral.

On the day of execution, Petronilla was the first to be taken from jail and tied to the stakes. Soon the flames crackled through the dry wood piled around her. She suffered in silence, but at last could bear it no longer. Her agonized screams echoed through the streets until they were ended by her death.

Then the mayor ordered the guards to bring forth Alice Kyteler. As their captain approached her cell door, he felt uncommonly hot and smelled smoke in the air. Was the cell on fire? Yes, the iron door was red hot! Guards fetched buckets and splashed water on the door as steam billowed out with a loud hiss, almost choking them.

When they tried to open the lock, the huge bolts would not budge. They called the blacksmith to bring his heaviest hammer. He pounded and pounded on the door until one of the iron hinges broke and the door fell inward. The guards rushed in, but the cell was empty. Alice Kyteler was nowhere to be seen. They looked up at the high window, but the iron bolts were in place. No one could have gotten out that way.

Now they summoned the bishop. He looked carefully

about, at the guards, the door, the cell walls, the window. He could not deny the evidence of his own eyes. And then he said, "Brethren, it seems to me that none other than the Old One has come for her at last. A true saying it is that the Devil knows his own."

The story of Lady Alice Kyteler comes down through Irish folk tradition and in some versions is far more elaborate. Modern research adds some interesting facts and theories. Hers was the first recorded case of a witchcraft trial on British territory. It took place in 1324, when witchcraft was accepted by the majority as a fact of life. It was taken as certain truth that the Devil was at work in the world and was freely helped by misguided men and women. The secular law laid down penalties for those who practiced the magic art of witchcraft, and religious law directed priests to destroy such heathenish evildoing.

One version of the story — contrary to the one told here — holds that Alice managed to escape to England, using her wealth and connections, *before* trial. Not Alice, but her alleged accomplice, the maid Petronilla, was tried. The maid denied everything at first. But after being flogged publicly six times, she confessed that while she herself was a witch, her mistress was a far more powerful one. She and her mistress had made magic charms for many purposes. Mixed in these charms were the brain of an unbaptized infant, herbs, worms, spiders, serpents, and the nails and hair of corpses. These were boiled together in the skull of a beheaded thief. This, she said, was how Alice had caused the unnatural deaths of some of her four husbands. The demon lover of her mistress was that dark man seen entering the house at night. He demanded that they sacrifice roosters for him at midnight at the crossroad.

One scholar suggests that Lady Alice got into trouble because of the great rivalry between her and the bishop. Her wealth and power gave her influence that he resented. Allying himself with her enemies, he launched the charges of witchcraft and murder that created turmoil in Kilkenny for years.

Some of Alice's accusers may have been angered by her personal wealth and ownership of property. She was a married woman, and at that time in Britain, marriage laws stated that a wife could not control land or money in her own name. Yet the much-married and much-widowed Alice was the richest woman in town. If condemned for witchcraft, her holdings would be confiscated and redistributed. Property was power, and that power belonged only in a man's hands, according to Lady Alice's enemies.

A search of the records suggests that Lady Alice's step-children may have started her persecution. Her husbands had brought their own children into the marriages, but in their wills had left substantial amounts of their property to Alice, and to Alice alone, cutting off their own children. The children's greed was reason enough for them to have accused Alice of witchcraft.

So it's clear why Alice Kyteler was accused of witchcraft. But why would her maid, Petronilla, confess that she herself was a witch? We know that she did not confess until she was publicly flogged six times. That fact is substantial indication of a forced confession.

The trial record admits it. Petronilla may well have undergone other forms of torture, as did countless others. Falsely accused, these unfortunates were tortured until they confessed. When you were accused of witchcraft, the tests you had to submit to left little chance to escape conviction and punishment. You could be tied hand and foot and tossed into a river. If you sank beneath the surface, it was a sign of your innocence. But the chances were you would drown before anyone tried to fish you out. If you floated, however, that proved you were the Devil's own instrument, rejected by God's water. And your punishment was swift and merciless. You were hanged on the gallows or burned alive at the stake.

There were other tests, too. In one, the Holy Bible was put on one scale, and you were put on the other. If the scales tilted to your side, it meant that your body was possessed by the Devil and that you were therefore a witch. In another test, you were hoisted into the air with heavy stones tied to your feet; you hung there till you confessed or your arms were torn from their sockets.

Witch-hunters might use thumbscrews or leg breakers to break your will. Or they would put you inside a hollow iron tube with spikes pointing inward that stabbed into your flesh whenever you twitched. They had no end of such devices.

Chapter Four

INNOCENT HAVE I BEEN TORTURED, INNOCENT MUST I DIE

IT IS HARD for us today to imagine what it was like to be the victim of a long-ago witchcraft trial; the records of such cases are written by the authorities, not by the victims. Yet we do at least have the record of how it felt for one innocent who went through its agonies. . . .

One of the most famous witchcraft trials in history occurred in the cathedral city of Bamberg, Germany, in 1628. The burgomaster, or mayor, of the town, Johannes Junius, was himself accused of witchcraft. The record of the trial is in the town library, which also contains a letter that Junius wrote to his daughter Veronica during the trial. The letter, which was smuggled out of prison, includes painful and moving details, and it suggests how little the official records convey the courage and suffering of witch-hunt victims.

Many hundred thousand good nights, dearly beloved daughter Veronica. Innocent have I come into prison, innocent have I been tortured, innocent must I die. For whoever comes into the witch prison must become a witch or be tortured until he invents something out of his head and — God pity him — bethinks him of something. I will tell you how it has gone with me. When I was the first time put to the torture, Dr. Braun, Dr. Kötzendörfer, and two strange doctors were there. Then Dr. Braun asks me, "Kinsman, how come you here?" I answer, "Through falsehood, through misfortune." "Hear, you," he says, "you are a witch; will you confess it voluntarily? If not, we'll bring in witnesses and the executioner for you." I said, "I am no witch, I have a pure conscience in the matter; if there are a thousand witnesses, I am not anxious, but I'll gladly hear the witnesses."

Now the chancellor's son was set before me . . . and afterward Hoppfens Elsse. She had seen me dance on Haupts-moor. . . . I answered: "I have never renounced God, and will never do it — God graciously keep me from it. I'll rather bear whatever

I must." And then came also — God in highest Heaven have mercy — the executioner, and put the thumb-screws on me, both hands bound together, so that the blood ran out of the nails and everywhere, so that for four weeks I could not use my hands, as you can see from the writing. . . . Thereafter they first stripped me, bound my hands behind me, and drew me up in the torture. Then I thought heaven and earth were at an end: eight times did they draw me up and let me fall again, so that I suffered terrible agony. . . .

And this happened on Friday, June 30, and with God's help I had to bear the torture. . . . When at last the executioner led me back into the prison, he said to me: "Sir, I beg you, for God's sake confess something, whether it be true or not. Invent something for you cannot endure the torture which you will be put to; and, even if you bear it all, yet you will not escape, not even if you were an earl, but one torture will follow after another until you say you are a witch. Not before that," he said, "will they let you go, as you may see by all their trials, for one is just like another. . . ."

And so I begged, since I was in wretched plight, to be given one day for thought and a priest. The priest was refused me, but the time for thought was given.

Now, my dear child, see in what hazard I stood and still stand. I must say that I am a witch, though I am not — must now renounce God, though I have never done it before. Day and night I was deeply troubled, but at last there came to me a new idea. I would not be anxious, but, since I had been given no priest with whom I could take counsel, I would myself think of something and say it. It were surely better that I just say it with mouth and words, even though I had not really done it; and afterwards I would confess it to the priest, and let those answer for it who compel me to do it. . . . And so I made my confession, as follows; but it was all a lie.

Now, follows, dear child, what I confessed in order to escape the great anguish and bitter torture, which it was impossible for me longer to bear. . . .

Then I had to tell what people I have seen [at the witches' Sabbath]. I said that I had not recognized them. "You old rascal, I must set the executioner at you. Say — was not the Chancellor there?" So I said yes. "Who besides?" I had not recognized anybody. So he said: "Take one street after another, begin at the market, go out on one street and back on the next." I had to name several persons there, then came the long street. I knew nobody. Had to name eight persons there. Then the Zinkenwert — one per-

son more. Then over the upper bridge to the Georthor, on both sides. Knew nobody again. Did I know nobody in castle — whoever it might be, I should speak without fear. And thus continuously they asked me on all the streets, though I could not and would not say more. So they gave me to the executioner, told him to strip me, shave me all over, and put me to the torture. "The rascal knows one on the market-place, is with him daily, and yet won't name him." By that they meant Dietmayer: so I had to name him too.

Then I had to tell what crimes I had committed. I said nothing. . . . "Draw the rascal up!" So I said that I was to kill my children, but I had killed a horse instead. It did not help. I had also taken a sacred wafer, and had desecrated it. When I had said this, they left me in peace.

Now, dear child, here you have all my confession, for which I must die. And they are sheer lies and make-up things, so help me God. For all this I was forced to say through fear of the torture which was threatened beyond what I had already endured. For they never leave off with the torture till one confesses something; be he never so good, he must be a witch. Nobody escapes, though he were an earl. . . .

Dear child, keep this letter secret so that people

do not find it, else I shall be tortured most piteously and the jailers will be beheaded. So strictly is it forbidden. . . . Dear child, pay this man a dollar. . . . I have taken several days to write this: my hands are both lame. I am in a sad plight. . . .

Good night, for your father Johannes Junius will never see you more. July 24, 1628.

Dear child, six have confessed against me at once: the Chancellor, his son, Neudecker, Zaner, Hoffmaisters Ursel, and Hoppfens Elsse — all false, through compulsion, as they have all told me, and begged my forgiveness in God's name before they were executed. . . . They know nothing but good of me. They were forced to say it, just as I myself was. . . .

Chapter Five

FROM FOLKLORE TO FRENZY

THE BIBLE of witch-hunting appeared in 1486 — just six years before Columbus set sail on his first voyage across the Atlantic. It was a book of great length called the *Malleus Maleficarum,* or *Hammer of Witches*. The first printed encyclopedia of magic and witchcraft, it was written by two Dominican priests of Germany, Heinrich Kramer and Jacob Sprenger.

Two years earlier, Pope Innocent VIII had authorized the two priests to wipe out witchcraft in Germany. Their manual on persecution was a tool in the hand of every judge and witch-hunter for three centuries. The *Malleus* was reprinted in fourteen editions very quickly. It became one of the most influential of all early printed books.

The *Malleus* begins by challenging the opinion that witches do not really exist. The true faith, it says, "teaches us that certain angels fell from heaven and are now devils" who "by their very nature . . . can do many wonderful things we cannot do." The authors state that Satan and the demons can do harm by themselves, or by acting with or through witches. In a single book, the *Malleus* pulled together many folk beliefs that up to then had been displayed only in local outbursts of witch-hunting. It dealt in much detail with the practice of witchcraft and with the judicial procedures to be used against it.

The two priests spoke from experience, for they themselves had tried fifty people for witchcraft, forty-eight of whom were women. The *Malleus* became the authoritative guide to organized witch-hunting. The hunts were initiated, financed, and carried out by church and state.

The priest or local judge was given the task of launching a witch trial. He would post a notice to "direct, command, require and admonish that within the space of twelve days . . . that they should reveal it unto us if anyone know, see or have heard that any person is reported to be a heretic or a witch, or if any is suspected especially of such practices as cause injury to men, cattle, or the fruits of the earth. . . ."

Any person failing to report a witch risked great punishment. If this notice exposed even one witch, her trial would be used to expose many more. The *Malleus* told how to use torture to force confession and further accusations. The common practice was to strip the accused naked, shave off all her body hair, subject her to thumb-screws and the rack, to spikes and bone-crushing devices, and to beat her and starve her.

People had long accepted that witches existed and did harm. In 1453, not long before the *Malleus* was published, an epidemic occurred in France, killing several children. The public blamed it on black magic, seized several suspects, and tortured them until five confessed and were promptly burned. In 1456, late-spring frosts ruined a crop of grapes. A boy said he knew who had caused it, and the people he pointed to were burned. In 1481, heavy rains damaged the vines, and nine women were executed for using witchcraft against the crop. In 1488, twenty-eight people were executed for causing a cold and stormy summer.

When the whirlwind of persecution descended in the fifteenth century, the toll was immense. Nicholas Remy, a judge from Lorraine, France, who presided over witch trials, wrote that after spending much time grilling witches, he knew that "they are justly to be subjected to every torture and put to death in the flames, both that they may expiate their crimes with a fitting punishment and that its very awfulness may serve as an example and a warning to others."

Remy sent between two and three thousand victims to

the stake between 1595 and 1616. He didn't limit his ruthlessness to adult suspects, either. He blamed Satan for so greedy a hunger for souls that he made use of the children of witches, too. He and other judges sentenced children to be stripped and beaten with rods in the public square where their parents were being burned alive.

In their fear of the Devil and his legion of witches, people like Remy ascribed wild powers to them. One man wrote that witches could move crops from one field to another — not by transferring the crops alone but by moving the fields themselves. Witches could supposedly make rivers run backward, solidify fountains, blot out the stars, and raise the dead.

But the judges didn't raise the dead; they created the dead. In huge numbers. Torquemada (1420–1498), the Spanish churchman known as the Grand Inquisitor, is credited personally with burning more than ten thousand people and with condemning another ninety-seven thousand in less than two decades.

For twelve years, from 1581 to 1593, witch persecutions raged through the cathedral city of Trier in Germany. The bishop of Trier, Peter Binsfield, ordered the death of some six thousand people. Upper-class people as well as commoners were among the victims. Years later, the clergyman Linden, an eyewitness, wrote down what he observed. He noted that the hysteria was encouraged by many officeholders and by others who profited from their victims' agony. Throughout the diocese, special accusers, judges, and constables dragged men and women to trial and tortured and burned them in great numbers. Meanwhile, Linden writes:

> Notaries, copyists and innkeepers grew rich. The executioner rode a fine horse like a noble of the court, and went clad in gold and silver; his wife vied with noble dames in the richness of her array. The children of those convicted and punished were sent into exile; their goods were confiscated. . . . A direr pestilence or more ruthless invader could hardly have ravaged the territory of Trier than this inquisition and persecution without bounds. . . . Many were the reasons for doubting that all were really guilty.

In the 1620s the area of Würzburg, Germany, saw spectacular examples of wholesale extermination. The bishop of Würzburg burned nine hundred people for witchcraft. They included a number of children, nineteen priests, and his own nephew. The archbishop of Trier burned 368 witches from twenty-two villages between 1587 and 1593. In two of these villages, by 1595 only one woman was left alive. Since women were most often identified with witchcraft, the cost to them was immense.

Jews were another group that suffered especially during

the height of the witch-hunts. In the New Testament of the Bible, John 8:44 calls the Devil the father of the Jews. It is in Revelation 2:9 and 3:9 that the "synagogue of Satan" is first mentioned. Church leaders accused Jews of worshiping Satan and giving their children to the demons. By the eleventh century, dissenters and heretics were being lynched by savage mobs. Soon after, the tales of Jewish atrocities became so common that Jews were particularly likely targets for the charge of witchcraft.

In France, in 1321, the rumor spread that lepers had plotted to poison wells and rivers. The charge was almost immediately extended to the Jews, who were accused of putting the lepers up to it. After burnings at the stake and other massacres, lepers were isolated, and the surviving Jews were expelled. Some twenty-five years later, when the epidemic called the Black Plague was raging in Europe, a similar accusation was made. This time the Jews alone had supposedly poisoned the waters and spread the plague.

In the late 1400s, the Spanish Inquisition accused Jews and Christian heretics of getting together to practice rites that were "contrary to Christian faith," a phrase that probably referred to the witches' Sabbath. This belief in a ritual of devil worship would be renewed time and again as people searched for a scapegoat on whom they could discharge fears, hatreds, and tensions of all kinds.

The Roman Catholic Church is often blamed for the persecution of witches, but the degree of its influence varied by country. In Catholic Spain, brutality was almost without limit, but in equally Catholic Portugal, the punishment for witches was not death but banishment. In England, under the Protestant rulers Henry VIII and Elizabeth I, persecution was severe. And they were not the only Protestant rulers to break bones on the rack or brand with hot irons. In the Netherlands, too, the whip, steel pincers, and burning at the stake were much in evidence.

Martin Luther, who lived from 1483 to 1546 and was the founder of Protestantism, reinforced the superstition of his time. His writings testify to the Devil's assaults upon him, and he often refers to the evil actions of witches — among whom he includes his opponents. He thought the power of witches was awesome; he once wrote, "I should have no compassion on these witches; I would burn all of them."

Spurred on by the *Malleus*, Germany had the worst history of witchcraft persecution, but other countries — France, Switzerland, Spain, Sweden, Scotland — all swelled the total number of murders. When the terror reached its peak, doubters felt obliged to voice a belief in witches. Denying the existence of witchcraft placed people in great danger of themselves being accused. This pattern is the major means by which mass movements of persecution happen — where seemingly good people become participants out of intimidation.

How did common folklore about demons and witches change into systematic persecution — climaxing in widespread horror that lasted for centuries? It's not easy to trace all the threads, and scholars in many fields still ponder the transformation. But they have marked out some important turning points.

Before the twelfth century, Christian thought had not developed a detailed picture of the universe, a blueprint of God's creation. Gradually scholars such as Thomas Aquinas began to consider both demons and witches to be part of the scheme of things. By the fourteenth century, there was an established body of investigators and judges whose sole duty was to uncover and uproot heresy, including witchcraft. By the fifteenth century, the witch was identified as the visible agent of evil on Earth.

And then there came the great social, economic, and political upheavals of the late Middle Ages and the Renaissance. Christianity broke apart into two warring camps — the Catholics and the Protestants. Terrible famine and plagues such as the Black Death destroyed populations again and again. These appalling disasters made people increasingly likely to blame their troubles on the force of evil and its demonic powers. And that belief in turn made the wholesale persecution of witches possible.

How could so many things go wrong? everyone wondered. It must have taken a vast host of demons, plus the witches whose services they commanded. This explanation fit in with the church's idea of an absolutely hostile, ruthless, and cunning Devil whose ability to injure humankind had grown tremendously. As fear of the Devil increased, so did the figure of the witch — his servant — become more frightening and more vile. Witches, church leaders and others concluded, had superhuman power to do harm to the faithful. These men portrayed witches as gathering in covens, feasting, and flying through the air on sticks or beasts to the blasphemous sabbaths where they met their master, the Devil.

The suffering that people believed witches caused them soon became a catalog of all calamities that people dread. Almost no one was immune to shattering anxiety. Seen in this light, the persecution of supposed witches was a desperate attempt to impose a system of thought on a bewilderingly unpredictable world — to restore order to chaos. Peasant, artisan, scholar, priest, layman, king, merchant — all believed in and feared witchcraft and called for ever more intense punishment of its practitioners.

Joan of Arc: Witch — and Saint

Accused witches were rarely executed in the Middle Ages. Though witches were strongly denounced, not many were killed. Punishments in the Middle Ages inflicted upon witches were limited to fines or some form of religious penalty. Not until the fifteenth century, when belief in witchcraft was well established all over Northern and Western Europe, did savage persecution begin. When that storm broke, it brought wholesale interrogation, torture, hanging, and burning.

The fate of Joan of Arc, who lived from 1412 to 1431, is one of the best known early examples of that deadly persecution. As we have seen, money and property were the root cause of the hounding of Alice Kyteler. With Joan of Arc, it was the fear of her military and political power that raised the cry of "witch."

Joan was the daughter of a farmer in France. Like most women and many men of her time, she could not read or write. But that didn't mean she was ignorant. She understood the political and military situation in France much better than most others did.

At an early age her imagination was so vivid that she heard voices and saw visions of saints. When she was about sixteen her voices urged her to help the dauphin, Charles, the French prince kept from the throne by the English during the Hundred Years' War between the two countries. Joan turned her great strength of mind and body to leading a soldier's life. She dressed in military clothing and, with enormous self-confidence, obtained an audience with the dauphin. Her belief in herself and in her voices was so overwhelming that she convinced the skeptical dauphin that she had a mission to restore him and France to their rightful place.

The dauphin supplied her with troops, who were inspired by her extraordinary spirit and military judgment. Although twice wounded, she won campaigns that ultimately saved her native France from the English invaders.

No wonder the English cried, "False enchantments and sorcery!" when Joan defeated them. They charged she had used the Devil's methods to gain victory over them. After being captured in battle, Joan was put on trial by the English and by some Frenchmen allied with England. She was accused of heretical acts — wearing men's clothing, cutting her hair short, and insisting she was answerable directly to God and not to the Church for her words and deeds. She was also accused of having been trained in witchcraft by the women of her native village and of listening to and obeying the voices of evil spirits.

Joan was imprisoned in a dungeon for a year and a week, chained by the neck, arms, and feet, or locked in heavy irons. When the court tried to force her to confess, she said:

> Even if you tear me limb from limb, and even if you kill me, I should not respond otherwise; and if I did speak otherwise, I should always thereafter say that you made me answer so by force.

Condemned by the court, at the age of nineteen she was burned at the stake. The wood was arranged so that the fire would consume her only very slowly.

A new trial twenty-five years after her death cleared her of all charges. And in 1920, Joan was elevated to sainthood by the Roman Catholic Church.

Chapter Six

WHY WOMEN?

HOW DID IT happen that women were the chief victims of the witch-hunts? Estimates of the number of women burned, drowned, hanged, and tortured to death between the fourteenth and seventeenth centuries range from five hundred thousand upward. Women were deliberately killed for all kinds of reasons. As one recent writer puts it, the victims were

> Women with freckles or a birthmark, old women, uppity women, women with property, women who were healers and who continued to pay tribute to Mother Earth and Goddess religions, women who were "in league with the Devil," women who today would be labelled mentally

> ill, women who enjoyed sex, a woman who resisted some man's sexual advances, and on and on and on. . . .

Looking back at the international record of witchcraft cases, the single most outstanding commonality is the gender of the victims. At least 344 persons were accused of witchcraft in New England between 1620 and 1725. Nearly four out of five were female. Of the men accused, about half were "suspect by association." That is, they were the husbands, sons, kin, or public supporters of accused women.

Centuries ago, woman had very little social or political power. While today there are women judges, jurors, sheriffs, and ministers, then there were none. Men held all the authority in the community. They had the power to decide the fate of the accused. And from the evidence, it appears they were convinced that to be a witch was to be a woman. If a woman was suspected of witchery, she was far more likely to be put on trial than a man, for the officials — all male — were very reluctant to believe rumors of witchcraft about men.

There was a double standard, too, in the treatment of suspects. In most places women were handled more harshly than men. Far greater pressure was put on women to confess to dealing with the Devil. Men who did confess were often called liars and dismissed, while most confessing women were taken at their word. Even if a man's confession was believed, he might only be whipped or fined or simply discharged after paying the jail costs.

It seems a man was considered much less dangerous to the community than a woman, though it was men who held power in church and state. Like any ruling class, however, they tended to protect one another.

While women bore a heavier burden than men during witch-hunts, not all women were equally vulnerable. It's true that women of all ages might be accused: the accused included women in their twenties, thirties, forties, and on up into their seventies.

But it was women over forty who were most likely to be persecuted. At the time of the witch-hunts, most people died before the age of forty, especially women, who frequently died in childbirth. A woman living into her fifties, sixties, and even seventies was automatically suspicious. She was too old to bear more children, and so she was considered no longer useful to the community. And if she limped or stuttered or was deaf or rheumy-eyed or couldn't get out of bed, she was especially to be feared rather than protected. Food and fuel were too scarce to waste on such a scary-looking old hag. Wasn't she clinging to life only to do the Devil's work?

In a society that believed in magic and witchcraft, people were suspicious of spells and curses that could do them harm. A woman's angry look: Was that the evil eye? Or her muttered swearword: Was that a curse? Or take the time of a plague. If they survived childbirth, women tended to live longer than men. Everyone saw that women recovered more often from plague than men. It was easy to suspect that women used witchcraft to survive. Or worse, to cause the deaths of the men.

In Christian creed, men and women are spiritually equal. But the apostle Paul and other church leaders held that women were the temptresses of men. Their influence is seen in the *Malleus Maleficarum*.

> What else is woman but a foe to friendship, an inescapable punishment, a necessary evil, a natural temptation, a desirable calamity, a domestic danger, a delectable detriment, an evil of nature, painted in fair colours. . . . [Women] are more credulous and since the chief aim of the devil is to corrupt faith, therefore he rather attacks them [than men]. . . . Women are naturally more impressionable. . . . They have slippery tongues, and are unable to conceal from their fellow women those things which by evil arts they know. . . . Women are intellectually like children. . . . She is

> more carnal than a man, as is clear from her many carnal abominations. . . . She is an imperfect animal, she always deceives. . . . Therefore a wicked woman is by her nature quicker to waver in her faith, and consequently quicker to abjure the faith, which is the root of witchcraft. . . . Just as through the first defect in their intelligence they are more prone to abjure the faith; so through their second defect of inordinate affections and passions they search for, brood over, and inflict various vengeances, either by witchcraft, or by some other means. . . . Women also have weak memories; and it is a natural vice in them not to be disciplined, but to follow their own impulses without any sense of what is due. . . . She is a liar by nature. . . . Let us also consider her gait, posture, and habit, in which is vanity of vanities.

According to the *Malleus*, women by nature are more evil than men. Created mentally, morally, and physically weaker, women are unwilling to accept their handicaps. And so they turn more readily to Satan to satisfy their needs. Women, the writers insisted, are more given to anger, jealousy, and greed, and therefore are ready to seek the Devil's power to deceive others and to draw them into evil.

Certain accusations against women appear often in the reports of witchcraft trials. Witches are accused of all manner of sexual crimes against men. As we saw in the *Malleus*, the church associated women with sex, and pleasure in sex was condemned because it could only come from the Devil.

Another common accusation against witches was that they exercised magical powers to affect health. They supposedly did harm, but, amazingly, they were accused of healing, too! An English writer of the witch-hunt era wrote that yes, there were "good witches which do no hurt but good, which do not destroy, but save and deliver." Yet, he went on, "it were a thousand times better for the land if all witches, but especially the blessing witch, might suffer death."

Midwives were often equated with witches. The *Malleus* had this to say about them:

> Midwives surpass all others in wickedness. When [midwives] do not kill the child, they blasphemously offer it to the devil in this manner. As soon as the child is born, the midwife, if the mother is not a witch, carries it out of the room on the pretext of warming it, raises it up, and offers it to the Prince of Devils, that is Lucifer, and to all the devils. And this is done by the kitchen fire.

People had long accepted that women who did farming or lived in the woods knew a lot about plants that made good food and about herbs useful for medicine. Their herbal remedies — such as ergot, belladonna, and digitalis — are still valued in today's pharmacology. Some women experimented to extend their knowledge of such remedies. They cured a neighbor's sickness by skill or by luck and thus earned a good reputation as well as some income. On the other hand, chance or ignorance could bring failure in the attempt to cure. And such a failure could be extremely dangerous in superstitious times.

Sometimes at trials for witchcraft, accused women said that local wizards had taught them professional midwifery and cures for illness. Such women were condemned no matter what the outcome of their treatment. If a midwife could bring both mother and child safely through childbirth, it was said she had called on the supernatural for help. But if either mother or child or both died, the midwife was accused of using her witch's power for evil.

One Englishwoman would have none of the widespread nonsense about midwives. In 1671, Jane Sharp, who had practiced the art of midwifery for more than thirty years, published *The Midwives Book of the Whole Art of Midwifery Discovered, Directing Childbearing Women How to Behave Themselves in Their Conception, Breeding, Bearing and Nursing of Children.*

Sharp showed profound knowledge of male and female anatomy and dispelled the superstition and myth surrounding the process of birth. She also argued that only women should be midwives because "the art of midwifery chiefly concerns us, which even the best learned men will grant." This book anticipated the Age of Reason, whose influence would soon reach Europe and the New World.

While the witch-healers practiced among ordinary folk, the upper classes relied on university-trained physicians. But in that day, such men — and they were all men, for women were denied entry to education — derived their prognoses more from astrology than from experimental science.

The assault upon women healers, labeled witches, gave these doctors a ready excuse for failure in treatment. If they could not cure someone, it was obviously the fault of witchcraft.

Chapter Seven

SHAKESPEARE'S WITCHES

Double, double toil and trouble;
Fire burn, and cauldron bubble.
Fillet of a fenny snake,
In the cauldron boil and bake;
Eye of newt and toe of frog,
Wool of bat and tongue of dog,
Adder's fork and blind-worm's sting,
Lizard's leg and howlet's wing,
For a charm of powerful trouble,
Like a hell-broth boil and bubble.

Macbeth, Act IV, Scene 1

WHAT ABOUT WITCHES in Britain, in the time of England's great poet and playwright William Shakespeare?

By the sixteenth century, Europeans were sure their continent was swarming with witches. England and Scotland suffered intensive witch-hunts during this period. Often dozens or even hundreds of witches were executed in a single town or region in a reign of terror that would last several years.

It's impossible to know the actual number of victims who were burned at the stake or hanged in Britain. Many researchers estimate the total at between fifty thousand and one hundred thousand, however, and some say that figure could be doubled or tripled.

During the reign of Queen Elizabeth I, from 1558 to 1603, the English of all classes believed in supernatural forces. These popular beliefs are reflected in the plays of Shakespeare, who lived from 1564 to 1616. Shakespeare makes frequent use of witches, ghosts, fairies, and demons in at least half his plays. Four of his works in particular — *A Midsummer Night's Dream, Hamlet, Macbeth,* and *The Tempest* — have much to do with the supernatural.

When Shakespeare was a child, witch trials received a great deal of attention. The Elizabethan law against witchcraft was passed in 1563, the year before Shakespeare was born. In the 535 cases of witchcraft presented under Queen Elizabeth, at least eighty-two women were executed.

Promoted by sermons, pamphlets, and ballads, the

antiwitch fervor led to horrifying charges. For example, in 1566 Elizabeth Francis confessed that she had been taught witchcraft by her grandmother, who had given her a white-spotted cat named Satan. The cat spoke in a strange, hollow voice, and Elizabeth fed it her own blood. She used the cat to harm her neighbors and then passed it on to another witch, Agnes Waterhouse, who did the same.

Another woman, Ursula Kemp, was accused in 1582 of "bewitching" three women to death. She reportedly used animal familiars to kill people and cattle. And in 1607 in Edinburgh, Isabel Grierson was executed for turning herself into a cat. Once transformed, Isabel broke into a neighbor's house and brought in a rabble of other cats and Satan himself, disguised as a black man.

A few people of that time doubted that witchcraft was real. Moved by curiosity, the French essayist Michel de Montaigne had gone to see an imprisoned coven of witches but found that the women were simply mad. A Dutchman, Jan Wier, published an argument denouncing the widespread belief in demons. He said that witches were mentally ill and explained their strange doings in medical terms. Similarly, in 1649, Gabriel Naudé decried the foolishness of believing that madwomen "had done a thousand childish, ridiculous, impossible extravagances for which they would better deserve to be healed or shut up in a madhouse than to exterminate them as one does by fire and rope."

In 1584, one brave soul, Reginald Scot, published an exposé of such beliefs, *The Discoverie of Witchcraft.* He wrote that belief in witches was a foolish superstition and that the punishment inflicted on women accused of dealing with the Devil was cruel and wicked.

The furious King James of Scotland ordered that all copies of Scot's book be rounded up and burned. In 1597, he replied to Scot with his own book, *Demonologie,* which was based upon his special study of European witchcraft. In his *Demonologie,* James told how witches can cause death by burning a person's picture, can make people sick by means of wax images, and can raise storms at sea or on land. His interest in witches was intensified after he sailed to Denmark to marry the Danish Princess Anne. On the homeward voyage with his wife, accompanied by Danish ships, they barely survived terrible storms. The Danes convinced James that the bad weather was to be blamed on witchcraft.

The Scottish people were harsher than the English. They burned some eight thousand witches in the forty years before James became king of Great Britain in 1603. Taking the throne Elizabeth had previously occupied, he had Parliament adopt a harsh law against witchcraft. That law of 1604 was enforced all through the seventeenth century in Britain and her colonies, including America.

James's law against witchcraft was far more brutal than the laws during Elizabeth's reign. In the first fifteen years of James's rule, the number of witches hanged each year was several times the number killed under Elizabeth's law of 1563. Throughout Elizabeth's reign, there had been disasters enough to make people believe some great evil was at work. The worst and longest period of famine in a century of bad harvests hit between 1593 and 1597. Just as that ended, the dreaded plague of the Middle Ages returned, killing one person out of five in London alone.

Shakespeare's works reflect the England of his time. In his plays, witches are usually portrayed as broken-down old hags who are given strange powers by the Devil. (Except perhaps in *Henry VI, Part I,* where he presents young Joan of Arc as a witch, who indeed was burned as a witch.) In the opening scene of *Macbeth,* the two Scottish generals, Macbeth and Banquo, are on their way to King Duncan's castle when they are startled by the sudden appearance of three witches. The witches tell Macbeth that he will become king of Scotland, and they promise Banquo that his sons will be kings, though he will never rule. The witches play important roles in later scenes, too. Macbeth is seduced by the evil that they embody.

Shakespeare wrote this play to please King James, who had come to the throne three years earlier and before whom the play was to be performed.

After his voyage from Denmark, King James took great delight in ferreting out women suspected of witchcraft. He threw them into prison, appeared at their trials, and took savage pleasure in grilling the victims himself. Under torture they confessed to performing the kinds of supernatural deeds that the witches in *Macbeth* boast of. A pain-crazed woman on trial admitted that she was one of two hundred witches who had gone to sea, each in her own sieve, in order to wreck ships.

Shakespeare took his notion of the three witches from a book called Holinshed's *Chronicles*. It was a history of Britain he mined as a source for his historical plays. Holinshed gave a vivid account of those "secret, black and midnight hags" meeting with Macbeth and Banquo, and Shakespeare's use of it confirmed the King's suspicion that old women sold their souls to the devil. When Macbeth accepts their help, he shares in their sins. He becomes caught up in criminal ambition and commits a terrible murder that leads to another and another.

Shakespeare's portrayal of the supernatural is somewhat different in *The Tempest*. In this play, humans have complete control over the forces of evil. Prospero, the noble figure who exercises potent magic, frees Ariel, a mischievous spirit, from the sorcery of Caliban's mother, the witch Sycorax, who learned her black magic from communion with the Devil. The depiction of witches has not changed, but Prospero, who also has command over spirits, never uses his power to do harm.

So how can we tell Shakespeare's own attitude toward the supernatural? If you examine it in the plays, it seems to vary a good deal. Perhaps one reason is that Shakespeare was just as familiar with Scot's book denouncing belief in witchcraft as he was with King James's defense of it. One of the modern Shakespeare scholars says the dramatist's view of witchcraft begins with "lighthearted, amused tolerance," changes to "serious meditation . . . and apprehension," and "emerges with a renewed faith and confidence in good." If only more people in England at that time had this humane and relatively tolerant view, less persecution might have taken place.

THE WITCHES' SABBATH

The witches' Sabbath was the great gathering of witches said to take place regularly under the leadership of the Devil. This notion of a hostile group (leper, Jew, witch) conspiring against society took shape in the mid-fourteenth century. The various covens were believed to congregate at night in meetings with the King of Evil, where he held court and handed out his favors. They met at a crossroad or in some wild and deserted spot, perhaps close to a swamp. Legend says that the ground became as barren as a desert, for once having been used for this evil purpose, nothing would grow there again. A favorite meeting place was said to be at the top of the Brocken Peak in the Hartz Mountains of northern Germany.

To prepare for the meeting, the witches were said to anoint themselves with oil from the fat and bone marrow of dead babies. Then they rode through the air on broomsticks or were carried to the meeting place by demons in the form of goats or asses, while other demons took their places at home.

Once all the devil worshipers had arrived, they faced the Devil, who was seated on a black throne in his favorite form — as a goat, with several horns jutting from his head, and a brilliant light shining out of one of them. He had a long tail, and his followers signified their allegiance by kneeling to kiss his hindquarters. Sometimes, however, the

Devil was said to show himself in the guise of a big black hound or an ox or the trunk of a tree. In one tale, he turns himself into little worms.

To make sure all present belonged to the master, the participants showed their marks. Novices were then pinched by an imp to make a blue mark that never disappeared and were also marked by the Devil as a sign of their loyalty. The marks were in the shape of a hare, perhaps, or a cat, a toad's foot, or a little black dog. Usually they were placed under the left eye and were made by the Devil's horns or else by his left claw.

Then the program began. The witches worshiped the Devil, shared in a great feast of stolen food, and offered sacrifices. Works of evil done by those present were reported and approved. Often there was music, and the witches danced with their little demons. The climax of the night's festivities was a great storm or tempest stirred up by the Devil. Then the witches gathered up their familiars, who had the form of small animals, and flew away home.

How did the witches' Sabbath get that name? It was done deliberately, to link Jews together with devil-worshiping witches. When Christianity became the state religion back in the early fourth century, the church insisted that Christianity was the true religion, the only religion, and that Jews must convert to it. When Jews would not give up their faith, the church used the power of the state to make them outcasts, a despised people, and to call them "devils cursed by God." Eventually, the term "Sabbath" — the seventh day of the week in the Jewish calendar, or the period from Friday evening to Saturday evening, which is observed as a day of rest and worship — became twisted to apply to the midnight assembly of the Devil with his witches. Sabbath is currently used by Christians to mean Sunday, their day of worship.

I Do Now Believe

The seventeenth century in England was so rich in literature that it would be hard to list all its poets, playwrights, and prose writers. This era saw the dawning, too, of great creativity in the sciences and mathematics. It seems extraordinary that such a flowering of culture went along with the belief in witchcraft, not just among ignorant peasants but also among educated people.

Protestant leaders such as John Calvin and his English disciples believed in Satan and declared that witches were his handmaidens. Calvin himself was prominent in organizing the killing of witches, citing the book of Exodus: "Thou shalt not suffer a witch to live." Sir Thomas Browne, a physician as well as an outstanding figure in English literature, said that "I have ever believed and do now believe that there are witches." Even Richard Baxter, an eminent Nonconformist minister, accepted their existence. So when King James, after seven years of research, published his book *Demonologie,* he was not running against the tide, but riding the crest of it.

Chapter Eight

WITCH-HUNT IN SALEM

IN 1620, a tiny band of English people, the Puritans, settled in Massachusetts. They brought with them the same laws that governed their home country. And one of those laws proclaimed death to anyone caught making a pact with the Devil.

Witch-hunting occurred in New York, Pennsylvania, and Virginia, but not with the frequency that it did in New England. There, the first witch to be tried and executed in the Massachusetts Bay Colony was Margaret Jones of Charlestown, in 1648. She was a healer and possibly a midwife. After this episode, however, many years passed before witch trials again took place.

Then, in 1692, a great battery of charges shook Salem Village (now Danvers), a few miles inland from the town of Salem proper. The cry of witchcraft affected not only Salem Village but also eight other communities in Essex County, Massachusetts, and Fairfield County, Connecticut.

Young girls ignited the witch craze by claiming they had been bewitched by two old women and by Tituba, a West Indian slave owned by the Reverend Samuel Parris. Within four months, hundreds of women and a few men were arrested and tried. The human toll was twenty executed (fourteen women and six men), and four others dead in prison. The lives lost were few compared with European witch-hunts. But the events in Salem Village still grip the American imagination.

The records of the trials give vivid testimony of how men, women, and children behaved in that time of great turmoil. It appears that in the winter of 1691–1692, children and young people were deeply interested in stories foretelling the future. Throughout Salem Village and the surrounding county, small circles of teenagers, mostly girls, were trying to predict the future by reading palms and were monkeying with "little sorceries." They experimented with sieves, keys, peas, nails, and horseshoes.

One of these little groups gathered in the Reverend Parris's home. Tituba, an uneducated, half-Indian, half-black woman, aged sixty, had demonstrated to the girls in her care some voodoo magic that had been part of her life in Barbados. The girls were Parris's daughter Elizabeth, age nine, and his niece Abigail Williams, age eleven. In turn, the children shared their secret knowledge with friends: Ann Putnam, age twelve, and Mary Lewis and Mary Walcott, both age seventeen. Still other friends joined the circle.

As they fiddled with fortune-telling, things got out of hand. They became upset and frightened. They began to act strangely: crawling into holes, creeping under chairs and stools, striking odd postures, making weird gestures, uttering strange chants that neither they nor anyone else could make sense of.

This went on for about two months, until adults began asking questions. At first the girls blamed no one for their spectacular fits. Then Samuel Parris asked William Griggs, the village doctor, what this wild behavior meant. The answer was terrifying: These girls are not ill from natural causes; they are in the grip of the "Evil Hand." It is the Devil's own witchcraft, he said.

When the girls were pressed to name names of who had bewitched them, the first person they mentioned was Tituba. But under repeated questioning, they began to identify a widening circle of villagers as witches. Most of these were middle-aged women, but men and even a six-year-old child were also accused.

We need to consider the state of mind of the villagers at the time the cry of witchcraft was raised. Not long before, the Native Americans of southern New England had made their last major attempt to drive out the white settlers, whose inroads on their lands and lives they bitterly resented. This bloody uprising was known as King Philip's War of 1675–1676. It destroyed twelve frontier towns. The rebel leader was captured and beheaded, and the Native Americans who surrendered were shipped off as slaves to the West Indies.

The whites justified the massacre and enslavement on the grounds that the Native Americans were pagan agents of the Devil. We colonists, wrote young Cotton Mather, "are a people of God settled in the Devil's territories." And the Devil, he said, is "engaged in this hellish design of bewitching and ruining our land."

From the earliest days of the settlement, Cotton Mather said, the Devil had waged his unholy war. He appeared in person to unfortunate Christians or through messengers from his invisible world and used bribes and threats to tempt Christians to enter his service. Whoever yielded to him was rewarded with supernatural power, secretly used for wicked purposes. These were the witches. Whoever resisted the Devil was tortured in mind and body almost beyond what any human could bear. And these were the bewitched.

In 1681, when the Native Americans resumed war, allied now with the French, the colonists were terrified.

Cotton Mather blamed the war on chiefs "well-known . . . to have been horrid sorcerers and hellish conjurors and such as conversed with demons."

The first person arrested for witchcraft in Salem Village was Tituba, the West Indian slave of Samuel Parris. Her accusers said she had dared to introduce the girls to the forbidden art of foretelling the future. And hadn't she mixed urine with rye to make a witch cake that could harm people? And what about the lessons she gave the girls in the dark of night in chanting and dancing? Wasn't that meant to give them magical powers?

What Tituba said on the witness stand was full of fragments of folklore and hardly intelligible, for she spoke very little English. She told of riding through the air on sticks, and said that Sarah Good, another of the accused, had ordered her to kill children. Tituba also said that a hairy creature had taken the shape of Sarah Osborne, another woman accused of witchcraft.

Tituba's testimony against others did her no good. The court saw her as the ringleader of the bewitched girls. They kept her in prison for eighteen months and then sold her to pay her jail costs. Interestingly, she was not executed.

Dorcas Good, a six-year-old, was brought in to testify against her mother, Sarah. She said her mother had promised her birds as familiars — one black and one yellow. Even though she testified against her mother, little Dorcas was thrown into jail for many months, starved, and chained. As the daughter of a convicted witch, in the eyes of the community, she was tainted, too. Spared the gallows, the child was driven insane by the ordeal and never recovered.

Some historians have linked the Salem witch trials to the painful changes the Puritan communities were undergoing at the time. The settlers of Massachusetts had entered the New World with a utopian vision of a peaceful communal life, but the temptations and pressures of commerce had overtaken them. Those who disliked what was happening felt a sad sense of moral loss. They responded with guilt and fear, blaming scapegoats for their troubles. Bitter quarrels broke out between factions within the village. Some villagers were more prosperous than others. And that may have helped to make the Salem witch-hunt the worst in the colonies.

So the trials went on, neighbor taking vengeance upon neighbor, and married men and women betraying each other. One couple — Martha Corey and her husband, Giles — was tried early in the witch-hunt. Martha had been named a witch by Tituba and the girls. She was the third wife of Giles, a much older man, now eighty-one. The crotchety Giles often quarreled with neighbors. Called as a witness at his wife's trial, he mentioned some peculiar behavior on her part, which the court took as evidence of her guilt. But on the stand, Martha showed open contempt for the trials and refused "to help find out witches." She said that witchcraft was nonsense, and when asked by the court if she had made a pact with the Devil to give him ten years' service, she laughed in the judges' faces. What about the children's charge that she kept a yellow bird as a familiar, and they had seen a strange, dark man whispering in her ear? Well, she replied, "We must not believe all that these distracted children say." A deeply religious woman, she called on God to help her. But the court showed no mercy, and she was hanged, along with four other women.

Two weeks after his wife's trial, Giles Corey was summoned and accused of acts of witchcraft against the girls and some neighbors. Young Ann Putnam said he had beaten, pinched, and almost choked her to death. Even while he had been in prison, she said, he had appeared to her many times and tortured her. Several of the other girls made the same charges. Adult neighbors gave evidence, too, that the old man made children so sick that they died. Giles stubbornly refused to recognize the authority of the court and remained silent. By law, if he denied the charge, his property would be auctioned off — but if he stood silent, his sons would have his farm. Angered, court officers tried to force him to confess by piling one great stone after another upon his chest, but all he would say was, "More weight!" Finally, he was pressed to death, his torture ended.

Another witch accused by Tituba and the children was Rebecca Nurse. She was a seventy-one-year-old mother of eight children, the wife of a farmer, and a church member. She was so sick that she scarcely ever got out of bed. And she was almost totally deaf. Those who testified against her said that she entered their houses, bit and pinched them, and tempted them to desert God for the Devil. When she moved her hands in court, the children would imitate her motion, cry out, and throw fits. But Rebecca Nurse swore before God that she was innocent and that at the times her accusers said she had come into their homes, she had never left her own house. If her accusers were bewitched, she said, it was not by her. The Devil, she said, might be appearing in her shape.

While awaiting trial, Rebecca was chained in prison for two months. Then the judges acquitted her. Yet her case was reopened when two self-confessed witches were brought into court to confront the old woman. "What, do these persons give evidence against me now? They used to come among us," Rebecca cried out. She was so deaf that she did not hear the court interpret her words as a confession that she associated with witches. Of course, she only meant that she knew the two people as fellow prisoners, not as witches.

Many people petitioned the royal governor, Sir William

Phipps, to release Rebecca. At first he was inclined to let her go, but he lost his courage and sent her to the gallows. What had counted strongly against her was an old tale that her mother had been a witch. The judges took the story seriously. Of course, the daughter of a witch must be a witch herself! And later, with blood ties taken as proof, two of Rebecca's sisters — Mary Eastry and Sarah Cloyse — were also tried and executed for witchcraft.

Two women, each of whom ran a tavern, were highly suspect because of their trade. Tavern keepers were lumped with witches in ancient folk belief. Bridget Bishop had been arrested and punished long before for lying and for stealing corn. Now, nearing seventy, she was hanged as a witch.

The other tavern keeper, Elizabeth Proctor, who was pregnant, was arrested around the same time. Her husband, John Proctor, was arrested the very next day when he came to court to protest his wife's arrest. He, too, was sent to the gallows, but his wife was allowed to plead her pregnancy and was granted a stay of execution. She was still in jail when the witch-hunt craze ended, but her husband's property was confiscated to pay the couple's jail costs. It was a life sentence of poverty and starvation for Elizabeth and her eleven children.

In other New England communities, pressure upon the accused was just as heavy — not only to confess but also to name others. In Fairfield, Connecticut, Goodwife Knapp was visited while in jail by several women who urged her to name any others she knew to be witches. But she replied, "I must not say anything which is not true. I will not wrong anybody. I must not render evil for evil." Just before she went to the gallows, still others tried to get her to name confederates, reminding her she was about to die. She burst into tears and said, "Never, never, poor creature was tempted as I am tempted; pray, pray for me." In 1653 she was executed, maintaining her integrity to the end.

Women who were considered to be troublemakers were prime targets for accusations of witchcraft. Anne Hibbins is but one of many examples. She and her husband settled in Boston in the early 1630s. He became a prosperous merchant and was elected to the colony's legislature. But bad times hit him hard, and his wife, who was said to be naturally crabby, became so quarrelsome that the church censured her. After William died in 1654, Anne's bad temper worsened, and some of her neighbors accused her of witchcraft. Her body was examined for the Devil's mark, and her belongings were searched for evil images and puppets with pins stuck in them. But though nothing was found, the miserable woman was condemned and executed in 1655. A prominent minister said years later that Anne Hibbins was "hanged for a witch, only for having more wit than her neighbors."

When brought to trial, many people confessed to witchcraft. Why? The court's central aim was to get a confession out of the accused, and they were often successful. Confessions at Salem Village came in great numbers — about fifty, by one count, pushing the craze to an even higher level. The confessions were largely the result of intense psychological pressure, applied when people were examined on the witness stand. If the accused person kept insisting on innocence, then the afflicted children who were present would go on displaying great agonies that became almost unbearable to observe. But as soon as the suspect confessed, the girls stopped their performance and even embraced and tearfully "forgave" their supposed tormentor.

But if the accused continued to claim innocence, it seemed to the accused herself, as well as to the onlookers, an unnatural and heartless act of cruelty. And thus to confess became a desperate way to end the girls' torment and to reenter the communal fold — at least for the moment.

None of the confessing witches was ever hanged. The court decided to keep them alive long enough to force them to give testimony against other accused witches who refused to confess. There would be time enough to execute the confessors in a group when their testimony was no longer needed.

Finally, a rising tide of opposition to the Salem trials and executions saved the lives of those women. It began with petitions on behalf of the accused. Sometimes as many as a hundred gave their signatures. Some people even had the courage to appear in court to give testimony favorable to the accused. And others in effect called the "afflicted girls" liars.

One witness even said that one of the afflicted girls had boasted to him that "she did it for sport." Despite the great personal risk, many honorable men and women were willing to speak out against the trials and executions.

Eventually, the leading ministers of Massachusetts, who had been cautious and uncertain for so long, took a decisive public stand against the witch-hunt. The Reverend Increase Mather, president of Harvard College (and Cotton Mather's father), addressed a meeting of ministers in Cambridge and then published his talk as an essay. He carefully examined the evidence in the cases and found it full of holes. In a single memorable sentence, he concluded, "It were better that ten suspected witches should escape, than that one innocent person should be condemned." A few days later, another of the colony's most influential men, the Boston merchant Thomas Brattle, published his own attack on the trials.

Now, with both the religious and secular leadership of the province united on the issue, it was clear that the hanging of witches in Massachusetts would end.

Within days, Governor Phipps announced that any further jailings for witchcraft were forbidden. A special court met to dispose of the remaining cases. The governor's order had eliminated the use of insubstantial evidence, the heart of most trials. The jurors then speedily acquitted forty-nine of the fifty-two cases. The three confessors who were convicted were given immediate reprieves. And three months later, the governor discharged all the persons still held and issued a general pardon.

The community was stricken with bad conscience over that terrible year of 1692. A public fast day of atonement was set by the legislature. And one of the judges, Samuel Sewall, stood up in his pew in Boston's Old South Church while his public confession of guilt and shame for his role in the trials was read from the pulpit.

Ann Putnam, a leader of the "afflicted girls," also repented publicly nine years later, when she joined the Salem Village Church: "I desire to lie in the dust," she declared, "and earnestly beg forgiveness of all those unto whom I have given just cause of sorrow and offense, whose relations were taken away and accused."

Even the jurors who had convicted those accused of witchcraft came to doubt and regret their decisions.

Twelve signed a public statement that they now felt the evidence was not sufficient to convict:

> We fear we have been instrumental, with others, though ignorantly and unwittingly, to bring upon ourselves and the people of the Lord the guilt of innocent blood. . . . We justly fear that we were sadly deluded and mistaken . . . and we therefore humbly beg forgiveness . . . and do declare we would none of us do such things again on such grounds for the whole world. . . .

Poison and Bewitchment

Was there a physical cause for the outbreak of witch persecution in Salem Village?

Yes, quite likely, in the opinion of recent researchers. They hold that microfungi — organisms too tiny to be seen by the naked eye — found in rye bread may have caused some of the symptoms that back in the seventeenth century were interpreted as bewitchment, or possession by the Devil.

Rye was cultivated in Salem Village and other

parts of Essex County in the late 1600s. The evidence suggests that witchcraft accusations in New England were prompted by an epidemic of ergotism, an ailment that no one at that time could recognize.

When a microfungi's poisons get into people's food, it may change their behavior. The ergot fungus thrives on homemade rye bread. Food contaminated by the fungus caused outbreaks of food poisoning, called ergotism, decimating many parts of Europe. The recorded symptoms include hallucinations, delusions, feelings of numbness or suffocation, panic, writhing, spasms, the "fits," blistering, and the sensations of being pinched, pricked, or bitten.

In the Salem witch trial records, other symptoms of bewitchment mentioned are typical of ergotism. These include temporary blindness, deafness, speechlessness, burning sensations, visions of "a ball of fire" or of "a multitude in white glittering robes," and the sensation of flying through the air "out of body." The "bewitched" girls said they felt they were being torn to pieces, with all their bones being pulled out of joint.

It's possible that some of the girls were merely imitating their friends' behavior. Yet this theory does not disprove the involvement of ergotism. Professor Mary K. Matossian, author of a study of the disease, says that ergot "is the source of lysergic acid diethylamide (LSD), and it may include natural alkaloids that act like LSD. People under the influence of this compound tend to be highly suggestible. They may see formed images — for instance, of people, animals or religious scenes — whether their eyes are open or closed. . . ."

Chapter Nine

CHILDREN: ACCUSERS AND VICTIMS

CHILDREN, too, played large roles in the witchcraft craze, in Europe as well as in America. Historical documents record children as both accusers and victims in New England and in many parts of Europe.

In one region of Sweden, great trials for witchcraft began in 1665. In all, eighteen death sentences were passed, with convictions resting largely on evidence given by children. In the end, seven of the condemned adults were beheaded and then burned, the usual form of execution for witchcraft in Sweden.

After these trials, the craze spread widely in Sweden, and several hundred children came forward to charge witchcraft. As a result, in another region, twenty-three people, mostly women, were sentenced to death. As the persecution reached into other communities, endless lists of children testified, and dozens of the accused were executed. Many little girls gave evidence against their grandmothers, mothers, and older sisters.

A few people protested against basing verdicts on the evidence of small children, especially when they concerned a death penalty. Others opposed the use of torture against "stubborn witches" and lamented the excessively large number of executions. But the officials replied, "The honor of God and the liberation and purging of the country from such a grave sin must be our prime concern. One cannot relax a rule in the face of mere quantity."

Even children who participated in trials applied a double standard. The great majority of those they accused of witchcraft were women rather than men, by a ratio of at least five to one.

Still, not until more than a hundred death sentences were carried out did some government officials begin to feel troubled by the children's accusations, which were often conflicting and uncertain. And then peasants began to petition the king to look into the witch-hunts. The end came when trials took place in Stockholm itself. For the first time, leading politicians and judges saw the hysteria for themselves. Suddenly, children began to confess that their stories were pure make-believe, and that the accused witches were innocent. Finally, a clear-headed scientist analyzed all the child testimony, and the witch-hunts came to an abrupt end. They had lasted eight long years.

What prompted children to act in this way? The Swedish witch-hunts have been studied by historians, psychologists, and sociologists. At their height, many children became professional witch-finders. They traveled from place to place and were paid for their services out of parish funds. Some children demanded food and drink from people in return for not accusing them. It was mostly poor orphans who combined begging with blackmail.

Those orphans emerged from a devastating time of war and crop failures in Sweden. Many people were made poor and hungry; they wandered over the land in search of food and work. Some desperate parents simply abandoned their children on the streets. Forced to survive on their own, the children found a place in the machinery of the witch-hunt. Although Swedish legal tradition did not allow persons under fifteen to act as witnesses in court, that practice was ignored during the craze. Children as young as five testified. It was common for twenty, thirty, or forty children to give testimony against the same witch.

As the trials went on, the more active children transferred their accusations to new suspects. A small core of boys and girls were responsible for most of the accusations, with the others following their lead. These organizers decided what details of evidence to give the next day in court. It was like the rehearsal for a play, with the director writing the script and coaching the performers.

While all this was going on, the Swedish aristocrats were cruelly indifferent. The upper class had grave doubts about witches or were openly disbelievers. Still, they did nothing to stop the trials. To them it was merely an amusing spectacle.

We've used Salem and Sweden as the major examples of the part children played in witch-hunting because they are so well documented. But evidence shows that children in other countries, too, were accusers, sometimes of members of their own families.

In a 1566 trial at Chelmsford, England, a sixty-three-year-old widow, Agnes "Mother" Waterhouse, was hanged for witchcraft on the testimony of Agnes Brown, a twelve-year-old girl. In 1612, in another English city, Lancaster, Jennet Device, a nine-year-old girl, gave testimony that led to the hanging of her own mother. In a 1692 trial in Salem, Massachusetts, George Jacobs was hanged on the testimony of his granddaughter, Margaret Jacobs. Later, she admitted her accusations were false.

Some nations did not hesitate to execute children

during a witch-hunt. In Mohra, Sweden, in 1670, fifteen children along with seventy women were executed on confessions of witchcraft. Another 136 children had to endure regular whippings for a year as punishment. When the Swedish witch-hunt came to an end, the courts prosecuted some of the most active witnesses for false testimony and executed them. Among them was a thirteen-year-old boy.

In Würzberg, Germany, in 1628, approximately three hundred children, aged three and four years old, were said to have had dealings with the Devil. And five children, aged seven, ten, twelve, fourteen, and fifteen, were put to death for witchcraft. Recall how in France in the same century, Judge Nicholas Remy declared that the children of witches were so infected with evil by Satan that they had "to be stripped and beaten with rods around the place where their parents were being burned alive."

But in the long history of witch-hunts, comparatively few children were accused of witchcraft. Witches were all ages, but the most common groups were those over fifty, probably in part because people believed that aging was supposed to increase magical powers. While children often acted as though they were possessed by the Devil — the Salem case is an example — they were not often charged with being witches. They were far more likely to be the alleged victims of witchcraft, an assumption that led to their accusing others of having bewitched them.

Studies of witchcraft point out that this is not surprising. Young children are easily frightened, and in accusing others of bewitching them, they do not understand, as adults may, the pain and harm they cause.

Chapter Ten

ADOLF HITLER: MASTER WITCH-HUNTER

THE SALEM witch-hunt was one of the last major witchcraft scares in the Western world. In Britain, forty-three years after Salem, the law against witches changed. The Witchcraft Act of 1735 said that from then on no person could be prosecuted for the practice of witchcraft. But anyone *pretending* to be able to cause any effect through magic was liable for prosecution. That law is still in effect.

The passage of the Witchcraft Act signaled a great shift in ideas and attitudes. Life had begun to change in so many ways that belief in witchcraft crumbled. Social, economic, cultural, and technological developments gradually shaped a modern worldview that made witchcraft appear to be incredible nonsense and superstition.

Popular beliefs, however, often lag behind the law. Even in the twentieth century, societies may be swept by movements that resemble the witch-hunts of earlier times. A group of people, whether by class, nationality, ideology, or religion, is singled out and accused of Satanic power and evil thoughts and acts. Often members of the group are publicly condemned, punished, or even killed.

That kind of persecution, a witch-hunt of vast proportions and with infinitely terrible consequences, began in twentieth-century Germany. Following Germany's defeat in World War I (1914–1918), the economy verged on collapse. The people were hungry and desperate. In such a period of dislocation and crumbling values, a community becomes insecure and frightened. As we have seen, people may easily be led to project their terrors upon certain individuals or a whole group, who can then be tortured and killed and so removed. The Germans looked for someone to blame for their disaster and for someone to lead them out of it.

They found their leader in Adolf Hitler, the head of a new political party, the Nazis. Something about him persuaded people to regard him as their messiah. He proclaimed that his party would create a new Germany, a Germany united on the racial principle that the Aryans, supposedly pure-blooded Germans, were the master race, born to rule the world. These supremaicist ideas became powerful political propaganda in Hitler's hands. He compared Jews to parasites on the bodies of other peoples. They were conspiring to achieve a world dictatorship, he claimed. The Nazis, he said, aimed to eradicate this alien race.

Hitler's anti-Semitism had ancient roots in the Christian Gospels, where the Jews were blamed for the crucifixion of Jesus. When, in the early centuries of Christianity, "Christ-killer" became a synonym for Jew, persecution inevitably followed.

For many centuries both church and state devised ways to harm Jews and assure their misery. They restricted which occupations were open to them, forced them to wear badges of identification, made them live behind ghetto walls, denied them access to education, and drove them to emigrate.

During the Crusades that began in 1096, Christians massacred Jews on a stunning scale. Later, when Martin Luther founded Protestantism, he tried to convert Jews. When he failed, he called the Jews poisoners, parasites, and devils. He urged the burning of their synagogues, the seizure of their books, and their expulsion from Germany.

In the early nineteenth century, a stream of anti-Semitic books and pamphlets began to pollute German culture, this time with a new twist: Even the baptized and assimilated Jew was held to be worthless, less than human. Now it was not religion that mattered but "race." The Jews' "race," their "blood," condemned them. And before the century ended, German philosophers were writing that Jews were "inferior and depraved." The duty of all Aryans, they wrote, was "to exterminate such parasitic races as we exterminate snakes and beasts of prey."

Hitler effectively used anti-Semitism to cement together such disparate elements as workers and industrialists, land barons and peasants, fools and intellectuals, atheists and preachers, young and old. Racial hatred became a magic formula to solve all social problems and a weapon against all opposition. Anyone who differed with Hitler was called a Jew or a tool of the Jews.

When Hitler won power in January 1933, he solidified his dictatorship over Germany and sowed the seeds of the Holocaust. As he prepared his people for a war of conquest, to extend Germany's control over Europe, he used every possible means to isolate and terrorize the Jews. There were only half a million Jews in Germany in 1933, less than one percent of the population. But according to Hitler, this tiny minority dominated industry, finance, and the government.

Hitler expelled Jews from the civil service, the army, the schools, and the professions. He took away their citizenship, restricted their housing, their shopping, their transportation, their every movement. His Nazis whipped up street violence against the Jews, beating and killing them. On Kristallnacht, the night of November 9–10, 1938, the Nazis burned most of Germany's synagogues, destroyed thousands of shops, and looted hundreds of homes. At least a thousand Jews were murdered and 26,000 were sent to concentration camps, which were slave-labor installations.

Less than a year later, Hitler launched World War II. During his attack on Poland, killing squads massacred captured Jews. Within a year, one to two million Jews had been killed. Confining Jews to ghettos in the countries overrun by his armies, Hitler exterminated still more people by starving them. As the war went on, the Nazis set up special concentration camps as slave labor installations. By mid-1944, that Jewish labor force was almost totally destroyed — by overwork, starvation, gassing and shooting.

When the deaths did not meet his schedule fast enough, Hitler speeded up the killing process by using Zyklon B, a gas that worked faster than monoxide gas. In Auschwitz and several other death camps, Jews were marched into newly designed killing chambers; they died within three to fifteen minutes as the gas poured in.

When the war ended in 1945, the processes of scapegoating and witch-hunting had accounted for the deaths of at least six million Jews in Europe.

The Holocaust: that is the term the Jews themselves chose to describe what happened to them during World War II. It was the most massive catastrophe in the 3,500-year span of Jewish history. Two out of every three Jews in Europe died, one third of the world's Jews.

The German code name for the systematic murder of the Jews was the "Final Solution of the Jewish Problem." Look at it in the light of the long history of witch-hunting and you can see, magnified many times over, the fatal outcome when people are accused of Satanic power and persecuted for alleged evil thoughts and acts. As was also true during times of massive witch-hunts, fear of being accused of being an enemy of the Nazis led ordinarily "good" people to fear for their own survival and become participants in persecution out of intimidation.

It is unfortunately true that when some leaders launch witch-hunts, many others may join in. Historians think that Hitler would never have succeeded in his mass murder of the Jews if he relied only upon ardent Nazis. Lawyers, doctors, scientists, engineers, professors, journalists, and ordinary working people lent a hand. When pressed after the war to explain their actions, they often defended themselves by saying, "I was just doing my job, just taking orders."

Chapter Eleven

WITCH-HUNT IN WASHINGTON

THREE HUNDRED years after the Salem witch-hunt, America experienced another dramatic surge of persecution, with wild charges, public trials, intense media coverage, and prolonged suffering of the victims.

It erupted in the early 1950s and is best remembered as the era of McCarthyism. The inquisition conducted under Senator Joseph McCarthy, however, was much greater in scope than what happened in Salem.

Behind the sound and fury of the McCarthy era was the conviction held by some that Communism — a set of economic and political beliefs more than a century old, calling for the overthrow of capitalism and its replacement by a collective society — was a danger that had to be crushed by any means necessary. In the United States, however, Communism has never been supported by more than a tiny minority. Americans in 1950 knew little about Communism, its strengths or its weaknesses. McCarthyism was possible because of fear and ignorance. Some politicians played upon this fear by crying "Red!" whenever dissent or protest was voiced.

The 1950s were not the first time the pumped-up threat of radicalism was used to sweep aside the Bill of Rights. After World War I, when the United States was beset by inflation and strikes, the real causes of those troubles were not examined. Instead, the weak radical Communist movement was made the scapegoat. A "Red Scare" erupted. Federal agents conducted raids in thirty-three cities and, in one night, netted more than five thousand "suspected" radicals. They were held for days, weeks, and months, to be deported "back where they came from" or jailed for twenty-year sentences.

Thousands of victims suffered terribly. But radical or not, they had a right to their beliefs. The postwar radicals were too weak and fragmented to be a threat to anyone. Yet the Department of Justice, instead of protecting the Bill of Rights, seriously undermined it by ruthlessly suppressing dissenters — people who disapproved of or differed with government policy.

By the summer of 1920, the wave of hysteria subsided.

The nation realized that the "Reds" were not about to overthrow the government. But fear and suspicion of radicals did not die out. The mood of that era seized the country again soon after World War II (1939–1945). Local, state, and national investigative committees raised the specter of a plot to overthrow the government by force or violence. They hauled in teachers, housewives, editors, actors, writers, and scientists and grilled them on their political beliefs and associations. By the time Senator Joseph McCarthy took center stage, the groundwork had been laid for his mammoth witch-hunt.

Joseph McCarthy was a senator, and he played on people's ignorance and fear, not for patriotic motives but to further his political ambitions. He began early in 1950 with sensational attacks upon the government for harboring alleged Communists in many of its departments and agencies. He accused the unnamed people of espionage and treason. But, strangely, he never seemed able to produce proof. Five investigations of his allegations were made by his Senate colleagues. But none of them led to a single conviction.

By making charges of Communist party membership against people in or out of government, McCarthy discovered he could dominate television time and the front pages. The media were a vital force in helping McCarthyism by playing up his accusations. Editors and broadcasters feared that to be critical of the senator would leave them vulnerable to accusation themselves. From 1950 until 1954, McCarthy used his immunity as a senator to ruin reputations, jobs, and lives. Running scared, government, business, and professionals hastened to set up security checks and blacklists.

Many people were disgusted by McCarthy's slander and his failure to prove anything. But for years few dared to speak out. The most powerful figures in public life were frightened by the prospect of tangling with McCarthy.

He found many allies in Congress. Some members of his own Republican party found it useful to let McCarthy tar the opposition Democrats with the Communist brush. And among the Democrats there were those who tried to neutralize his attacks by joining in the hunt for alleged radicals.

The first to challenge McCarthy was the only woman in the Senate at that time, Margaret Chase Smith of Maine. She had kept silent for months, expecting McCarthy to produce some solid evidence. But as his accusations grew ever more reckless, she took the Senate floor. In firm tones she said to the quiet, crowded chamber:

> I think it is high time for the United States Senate to do some real soul-searching. . . . Those of us who shout the loudest about Americanism in making

> character assassinations are all too frequently those who, by our own words and acts, ignore some of the basic principles of Americanism —
>
> The right to criticize.
>
> The right to hold unpopular beliefs.
>
> The right to protest.
>
> The right of independent thought.
>
> The exercise of those rights should not cost one single American citizen his reputation or his right to a livelihood, nor should he be in danger of losing his reputation or livelihood merely because he happens to know someone who holds unpopular beliefs. Who of us does not? Otherwise none of us could call our souls our own. Otherwise thought control would have set in.
>
> The American people are sick and tired of being afraid to speak their minds lest they be politically smeared as Communists or Fascists by their opponents. Freedom of speech is not what it used to be in America. It has been so abused by some that it is not even exercised by others. . . .

But McCarthy only sneered at Senator Smith's speech. And with the election of Republican president Eisenhower in 1952, McCarthy became the head of his own Senate committee with the power to investigate every branch of the executive arm of government.

By piling accusation on accusation, McCarthy led the media and the public by the nose, dominated Congress, and terrorized the executive arm of government. More than seven thousand federal workers were fired as "security risks" by frightened officials anxious to appease the senator. He called Harvard and Yale "sanctuaries" for radical professors and made teachers everywhere afraid to discuss public issues in their classrooms. Heresy hunters took McCarthy's cue and censored textbooks and libraries. Books that the senator criticized were even burned in U.S. libraries overseas.

Like Hitler, McCarthy exploited popular fears. After four years of unproved charges, the Gallup Poll reported that fifty percent of the American people had a generally "favorable" opinion of him. Only twenty-nine percent had an unfavorable one, and twenty-one percent had no opinion. No wonder that Supreme Court Chief Justice Earl Warren felt such despair. He said that if the Bill of Rights were put to a vote, it would lose.

Just as in Salem long before, some people testified against the modern "witches," naming names of people who in turn were dragged into the hearings and urged to name names of still others. One informer named a thousand people, others 482, or 450, 411, or 318 — providing the oil needed to keep the machinery of exposure running smoothly. As in early witch trials, such testimony became the main way for the accused to win pardon for their own "sins" and be restored to the good graces of the community.

Other people, however, resisted the grilling of whatever committee they appeared before. Depending upon their course of action, some were cited for contempt and served a year in prison. Others, who pleaded the right to remain silent — the Fifth Amendment — escaped jail but were disgraced in the eyes of the press and the public. They lost their jobs, their trades, their professions, their businesses. Almost no one would hire them, and few would even be seen talking to them. Their lives and their families' lives became a torment.

Was that system of exposure used by McCarthy and other committees much different from the Inquisition and the witch trials? The aim was the same, and the destroyed lives that resulted can be compared to the pillory, the slicing off of ears, the sentences to prison, the long exile. The victims were heretics, nonconformists, dissenters to be shunned by society.

As for McCarthy himself, he eventually did harm to the Eisenhower administration, especially when he attacked the U.S. Army for harboring "Reds." A special congressional investigating committee held hearings in 1954 that exposed the senator as a blustering bully, and his power disappeared almost overnight. Three years later he was dead.

The anti-Communist frenzy of the McCarthy era illustrates how fear can be mobilized against a demonized enemy. Dissenters were made the witches of the 1950s, and severe punishments were meted out to them. True, there were no mass executions. But as we've seen, freedom of speech was savaged, thousands lost their jobs, some committed suicide, and others died of heart attacks under the shock of public humiliation. This witch-hunt, too, damaged trust within American society.

Why the Craze?

One historian of witchcraft, Professor Jeffrey B. Russell, holds that a witch craze is not the fault of a particular social crisis or set of ideas. It can't be blamed essentially on the Middle Ages or Christianity or Renaissance magic. His study of witch crazes leads him to the conclusion that a witch craze occurs because of a negative aspect of human nature: "the desire of human beings to project evil on others, define them as outsiders, and then punish them horribly."

Take the burnings at Bamberg, the hangings at Salem, and compare them to the ovens at

Auschwitz, the American soldiers' massacre of Vietnamese civilians at My Lai during the twentieth-century Vietnam War, or the brutalities of Stalin's treatment of prisoners in the Soviet labor camps. They are made possible by essentially the same element in human nature, Russell believes. He is convinced that the specific form a craze may take is determined by the circumstances of the times, "but the evil lurking behind the form is independent of ideologies."

Chapter Twelve

WITCHES TODAY

WHAT ABOUT witchcraft today?

Many fear witchcraft now as much as their ancestors did during earlier times. And others are now calling themselves modern witches.

The age-old belief in hostile spirits is a universal human experience. And despite what science and psychology have done to explore the unknown and make the existence of evil spirits seem improbable, people still suffer the feeling of something alien and terrible crossing into their everyday world. The fears of some are magnified by the powerful influence of sensational newspaper stories, movies, and television shows. These picture strange characters practicing weird and often bloody rites.

Now and then reports appear of people charged with harming others in cult rituals associated with witchcraft, or, as it is now often referred to, Satanism. In recent years people have been convicted of Satanic ritual abuse or murder of children. In Virginia, vandalism of a mausoleum was said to indicate Satanism. In Los Angeles, a man charged in a hatchet murder was suspected of committing the crime as a human sacrifice. In Arkansas, three teenage boys were charged with the murders of three eight-year-old boys, in a crime rumored to be part of a Satanic cult ritual. In Maryland, a man was indicted for breaking into an Orthodox Jewish school and vandalizing it. It was reported that he was an avowed Satanist.

In Montana, a school librarian was fired for lending — with the permission of their parents — two of her own books to two girls who were doing reports on witchcraft in the Middle Ages. In Texas, a fourth-grade teacher was criticized for assigning reading material some parents felt might expose their children to Satanism.

The fear of Satanism has led in some places to the banning of the traditional Halloween celebration. The holiday is now seen by some religious leaders as an expression of witchcraft. They say the holiday is grounded in Satanic ritual or that it has lost whatever innocence it once had. A number of schools, churches, and communities have been persuaded to drop the celebration or to alter it drastically.

In other parts of the world, fears about witchcraft are having truly horrifying effects. In South Africa, with the ending of apartheid and the dawning of democracy, a passion for witch-hunting seized people in rural areas. In 1994, at least one hundred women were accused of witchcraft and were burned or stoned to death. In some cases their own husbands or children were the accusers. Investigators said that with the end of the conflict over the separation of the races, troubling superstitions of the past seem to have revived, reflecting clashes between traditional and modern beliefs. Beginning in 1992 in Kenya, another African country, dozens of men and women were burned to death because of accusations that they were practicing witchcraft.

These sorts of news stories have led, in the United States, to a mounting fear, among some, of the forces of evil and of anything related to witchcraft. But in fact, if a very few people do worship Satan or the Devil and harm others as part of their cult rituals, they have little in common with the modern practice of witchcraft, or Paganism, as it is also called.

Paganism is a way of life for many people in America and abroad. These people come from all walks of life and are very diverse in class and ethnic background. They find common ground in a religion that encourages love of the Earth and reveres what they consider to be the feminine aspect of the divine. Contrary to common opinion, their religious observances are neither evil nor destructive. They have nothing to do with devil worship, Satanism, human sacrifice, or orgies. Through their rituals, Pagans aim to draw upon natural energies found, they believe, in the Earth and within their bodies, to create life-affirming change.

The word "pagan" generally means a religion that does not revolve around a single, central deity, but that preaches the existence of many gods or no gods at all. Today, those who call themselves Pagans or Neo-Pagans consider themselves a part of a religious movement that reaches back to a time long before the deistic faiths of Judaism, Christianity, or Islam were developed. There are hundreds, perhaps thousands, of groups in this movement. Some have only a few members, others have several hundred.

Margot Adler, who has studied witches and Pagans and their beliefs in America for many years, writes that these groups:

> are often self-created and home-made, they seldom have "gurus" or "masters"; they have few temples and hold their meetings in woods, parks, apart-

> ments, and houses; in contrast to most organized cults, money seldom passes from hand to hand and the operations of high finance are nonexistent; and entry into these groups comes through a process that could rarely be called "conversion."

Although unusual, modern Paganism can be seen as a valid expression of the religious experience. Religions as well as the sciences have wrongly taught that Paganism is only nonsense involving the worship of idols or silly gods, or belief in irrelevant myths. In fact, when the religions of Egypt, Canaan, the Celts, and Teutons are respectfully studied, we find they are rich, beautiful, and full of insight. Today's Neo-Pagan groups are trying to re-create the positive aspects of these historical Pagan religions.

These groups stress certain values they feel are particular to the Pagan tradition. They celebrate creativity in personal expression. There is openness toward poetry, dance, music, laughter, and spontaneity. Because witchcraft in their sense is a term covering many forms of creativity, the groups are only loosely connected. No one form or belief dominates or controls.

Another important principle for Neo-Pagans is polytheism — the belief that there are many gods. This of course differs from the majority tradition of monotheism

— belief in one God. The idea of polytheism emerges from the view that reality (divine or otherwise) is multiple and diverse. That belief allows all the different groups of Neo-Pagans to coexist in harmony for the most part, even though they may differ greatly in some of their beliefs and practices.

Finally, Neo-Pagans believe that all nature is divine. Modern witchcraft includes a sense of awe toward the natural world and love and reverence for the universe. Most Neo-Pagan groups are not opposed to science and technology but only to their abuse.

Why the word "pagan"? It comes from the Latin *paganus,* meaning a country dweller. It has a negative connotation for many because by the time Christianity became a major religion in the Roman Empire, the church used it as a term for contempt for the country folk who still clung to the older, polytheistic religions. It came to mean a godless person or an unbeliever. The truth was, such persons were simply believers in a pre-Christian nature religion.

And what about the words "witch" and "witchcraft"? Their root is in the Old English *wicce* and *wicca,* meaning female or male practitioner. Modern dictionaries define a witch as primarily a woman, either lovely and seductive ("bewitching") or ugly and evil ("wicked") and endowed with "supernatural" powers. But in the current revival of Paganism or witchcraft, the word "witch" means an initiate of the religion called Wicca, also often called the Craft.

As for the word "religion," Neo-Pagans note that at its root, the word means "to relink," "to connect." As with other religions, theirs strives for deep connections between human beings and the universe.

In the view of many, the social order of our world has begun to crack. Existing forms of community life fail to satisfy people's needs for order and security. In the twentieth century, endless warfare, revolutions, mass poverty, and hunger have ravaged the world. The hold of traditional religious, psychological, and philosophical beliefs has weakened. To find answers to troubling questions about the world, some people have determined to cling even more tightly to traditional religions and ideas and to look for others to blame and persecute. Others, including the Neo-Pagans, are open to new or alternative ways of looking at the world.

Though modern witches are perhaps few in number, the efforts of such groups to find their own path to a meaningful life merits our respect and certainly our tolerance. As one anonymous witch put it, "Worship as you see best, and allow us also the same right."

For no one deserves to be the target of a witch-hunt, not even those who today call themselves witches.

AFTERWORD

STORIES OF witchcraft and witch-hunts fascinate almost everyone. Here is the strange, the dark side of life. Something about this history touches us deeply. What does it mean? How does it affect us?

That the stories told in this book extend back into antiquity and forward into today's world suggest how powerful the fascination is. What can we learn from this history?

Reading these accounts casts light on human behavior in times of great stress. We find that damaging patterns of behavior like witch-hunting are common to people in cultures of many different kinds and in all parts of the world, including our own communities.

Everywhere the danger of making scapegoats of

innocent people is painfully clear. Crazed behavior can erupt when unscrupulous leaders manipulate public opinion to enlarge their power. It can result in great harm — pain, torture, imprisonment, and even death — for hundreds, thousands, millions.

But the tales of witchcraft and witch-hunts do not simply illuminate the evil humankind is capable of. They also bring home the good inherent in those with courage and compassion, those men and women who speak out when they see cruelty and injustice done to their fellow beings.

NOTES

Items in the Bibliography are referred to here by the last name of the author.

Chapter One

The tale of Agnes Waterhouse is from Radford. The European myths about witchcraft are treated in the splendidly detailed volume edited by Ankarloo. It contains scientific papers presented at an international witchcraft symposium in Stockholm in 1984. Scholarship up to that time had focused largely on Western Europe. I made use of the eighteen papers, written by men and women from many countries, throughout this book. Other sources for this chapter are Cavendish, Kors, and Leach.

Chapter Two

References to witches in world literature and myth are found in the Bible's Old and New Testaments, Kors's documentary history, Shah's treatment of the occult in many cultures, the *Odyssey*, the *Aeneid*, Brandsted, and Cavendish.

Chapter Three

The story of Alice Kyteler is among the many witch tales in Lenihan, but scraps of information about her are also scattered in several other books, including Peters, Shah, and Williams.

Chapter Four

The text of the letter from prison by Johannes Junius to his daughter is found in Kors.

Chapter Five

The handbook of witchcraft — *Malleus Maleficarum* — is quoted from and discussed in a great many books. I used Ankarloo, Cavendish, Kors, Leach, Peters, Shah, and Williams for material on the witch craze in Europe.

Chapter Six

Ehrenreich is only a forty-five page pamphlet, but it is crammed with facts and voices a feminist view. Russell has much on women as victims in several periods of persecution, but Williams was my chief source.

Almost half of Williams's book is given to an analysis of the Salem craze from the standpoint of a feminist historian. Wendell and Silverman discuss the role of Cotton Mather. Hall's documentary history contains some fifty pages of documents and a selective bibliography on the witch-hunts of that period. Hall's *Worlds of Wonder* probes the elements in Puritan life as well as the social and economic factors that contribute to an understanding of the craze. Matossian reports on the microfungi that cause symptoms like those manifested by the young girls in the Salem trials.

Chapter Seven

The many references to witches in several of Shakespeare's plays are, of course, found in the texts. Cavendish discusses witch tales current in the playwright's time; Ankarloo links James I to Denmark; the King's *Demonologie* is discussed in Williams, as is Reginald Scot's book. The role of witches in the plays is in Levi and Wills and in the indispensable, encyclopedic treatment of Shakespeare in Campbell.

Chapter Eight

The events in Salem Village of the 1690s have commanded great attention from many generations of scholars. The difficult task of compiling and transcribing the legal documents was carried out by the staff of the Works Progress Administration in 1938. (The WPA was one of the many New Deal agencies that made great contributions not only to America's infrastructure but to its cultural life.) The records were first published in 1977 by Da Capo Press, in three volumes edited by Boyer and Nissenbaum. These are immensely valuable to anyone interested in the phenomenon of the witch-hunt. I made full use of the documents and of the keen analysis of them in the editors' introduction.

Chapter Nine

Ankarloo, Kors, and Russell are the chief sources on children as accusers and children as victims.

Chapter Ten

My *Never to Forget* encompasses the details of the step-by-step development of the Holocaust and provides analysis based upon the findings of many scholars as well as the first-person testimony of the victims. Russell offers comparisons of various witch crazes and links them to one aspect of human nature.

Chapter Eleven

Many studies have been made of the McCarthy era as an example of twentieth-century witch-hunts. I relied on Kovel, Levy, Marwick, Russell, and my own book on the Fifth Amendment, which deals with the inquisition of the mid-twentieth century.

Chapter Twelve

Adler, in the revised and expanded 1986 edition, is among the foremost authorities on Neo-Paganism today. Her six-hundred-page study is a healthy corrective to many common misconceptions. Besides the insights gathered from extensive interviews and surveys carried out personally over several years, she provides a resource guide to newsletters, journals, books, groups, and festivals. I also used Buckland, Eliade, Goodman, Marwick, Parker, and Wright. The incidents of contemporary Satanism are taken from reports appearing in the press during the years 1992, 1993, and 1994.

BIBLIOGRAPHY

Adler, Margot. *Drawing Down the Moon: Witches, Druids, Goddess-Worshippers, and Other Pagans in America Today*. Boston: Beacon Press, 1986.

Ankarloo, Bengt, and Gustav Henningsen, eds. *Early Modern European Witchcraft*. New York: Oxford University Press, 1989.

Barstow, Anne Llewellyn. *Witchcraze: A New History of the European Witch Hunts*. New York: Pandora, 1994.

Boyer, Paul, and Stephen Nissenbaum, eds. *The Salem Witchcraft Papers*. 3 vols. New York: Da Capo Press, 1977.

Brandsted, Johannes. *The Vikings*. Baltimore: Penguin Books, 1967.

Breslaw, Elaine G. *Tituba: Reluctant Witch of Salem: Devilish Indians and Puritan Fantasies*. New York: New York University Press, 1996.

Buckland, Raymond. *The Tree: The Complete Book of Saxon Witchcraft*. York Beach: Samuel Weiser, 1974.

Campbell, James, ed. *The Readers Encyclopedia of Shakespeare*. New York: Crowell, 1966.

Cartwright, Frederick F., with Michael D. Biddiss. *Disease and History*. New York: Dorset House Publishing, 1972.

Cavendish, Richard. *The Powers of Evil in Western Religion, Magic and Folk Belief*. New York: Dorset House Publishing, 1975.

Cunningham, Scott. *The Truth About Witchcraft Today*. St. Paul: Llewellyn Publications, 1993.

Ehrenreich, Barbara, and Deirdre English. *Witches, Midwives, and Nurses: A History of Women Healers*. New York: The Feminist Press, 1973.

Eliade, Mircea. *Occultism, Witchcraft, and Cultural Fashions*. Chicago: University of Chicago Press, 1976.

Ginszburg, Carlo. *The Night Battles*. Baltimore: Johns Hopkins University Press, 1992.

Goodman, Felicitas D. *How About Demons? Possession and Exorcism in the Modern World*. Bloomington: Indiana University Press, 1988.

Guiley, Rosemary Ellen. *The Encyclopedia of Witches and Witchcraft*. New York: Facts on File, 1990.

Hall, David D., ed. *Witch-Hunting in Seventeenth Century New England: A Documentary History, 1638–1692*. Boston: Northeastern University Press, 1991.

Hall, David D. *Worlds of Wonder, Days of Judgement: Popular Religious Belief in Early New England*. Cambridge: Harvard University Press, 1989.

Hansen, Chadwick. *Witchcraft at Salem*. New York: George Braziller, 1969.

Hoffer, Peter Charles. *The Devil's Disciples: Makers of the Salem Witchcraft Trials*. Baltimore: Johns Hopkins University Press, 1996.

Karlsen, Carol F. *The Devil in the Shape of a Woman: Witchcraft in Colonial New England*. New York: Vintage Books, 1989.

Kaye, Marvin, ed. *Witches and Warlocks: Tales of Black Magic Old and New*. New York: Barnes & Noble Books, 1989.

Kennedy, Patrick. *Legends of Irish Witches and Fairies*. Dublin: Mercier Press, 1976.

Kors, Alan C., and Edward Peters, eds. *Witchcraft in Europe: A Documentary History 1100–1700*. Philadelphia: University of Pennsylvania Press, 1972.

Kovel, Joel. *Red Hunting in the Promised Land: Anti-Communism in the Making of America*. New York: Basic Books, 1994.

Lea, Henry Charles. *The Inquisition of the Middle Ages*. London: Eyre & Spottiswoode, 1963.

Leach, Maria, ed. *Standard Dictionary of Folklore, Myth and Legend*. New York: Funk and Wagnalls, 1972.

Lenihan, Edmund. *Ferocious Irish Women*. Dublin: Mercier Press, 1991.

Lerner, Gerda. *The Creation of Feminist Consciousness*. New York: Oxford University Press, 1993.

Levi, Peter. *Life and Times of William Shakespeare*. New York: Holt, 1988.

Levy, Leonard W. *Origins of the Fifth Amendment*. New York: Oxford University Press, 1968.

Maloney, Clarence, ed. *The Evil Eye*. New York: Columbia University Press, 1976.

Marwick, Max, ed. *Witchcraft and Sorcery: Selected Readings*. New York: Penguin Books, 1990.

Matossian, Mary Kilbourne. *Poisons of the Past: Molds, Epidemics, and History*. New Haven: Yale University Press, 1989.

Meltzer, Milton. *Never to Forget: The Jews of the Holocaust*. New York: HarperCollins, 1976.

Meltzer, Milton. *The Right to Remain Silent*. New York: Harcourt, 1972.

Murray, Margaret A. *The Witch-Cult in Western Europe*. New York: Barnes & Noble Books, 1996.

Newall, Venetia, ed. *The Witch in History*. New York: Barnes & Noble Books, 1996.

Parker, John. *At the Heart of Darkness: Witchcraft, Black Magic and Satanism Today*. New York: Citadel Press, 1993.

Peters, Edward. *The Magician, the Witch, and the Law*. Philadelphia: University of Pennsylvania Press, 1978.

Radford, Ken, ed. *Fireburn: Tales of Witchery*. New York: Wings, 1989.

Reis, Elizabeth. *Damned Women: Sinners and Witches in Puritan New England*. Ithaca: Cornell University Press, 1998.

Rosenthal, Bernard. *Salem Story: Reading the Witch Trials of 1692*. New York: Cambridge University Press, 1998.

Russell, Jeffrey B. *A History of Witchcraft: Sorcerers, Heretics and Pagans*. New York: Thames and Hudson, 1980.

Shah, Sirdar Ikbal Ali. *Occultism: Its Theory and Practice*. New York: Dorset House Publishing, 1993.

Silverman, Kenneth, ed. *Lifetimes of Cotton Mather*. New York: Columbia University Press, 1985.

Weber, Eugen. *A Modern History of Europe: Men, Cultures and Society from the Renaissance to the Present*. New York: W. W. Norton & Company, 1971.

Wendell, Barrett. *Cotton Mather*. New York: Barnes & Noble Books, 1992.

Williams, Selma R., and Pamela Williams Adelman. *Riding the Nightmare: Women and Witchcraft from the Old World to Colonial Salem*. New York: HarperCollins Publishers, 1992.

Wills, Garry. *Witches and Jesuits: Shakespeare's Macbeth*. New York: Oxford University Press, 1995.

Wright, Lawrence. *Remembering Satan*. New York: Alfred A. Knopf, 1994.

INDEX